Togetherness Redefined

Togetherness Redefined:

Finding a Different Kind of Family Togetherness

Celeste Orr

Togetherness Redefined
Finding a Different Kind of Family Togetherness
togethernessredefined.com

For Matthew,

who's been making me smile
since 1996,

who sees me
when I can't see myself,

who constantly reminds me
not to take this life so seriously,

who loves me
more than I knew I could be loved.

This one's for you.

Table of Contents

Introduction

So Nice to Meet You

"Happiness is going to bed knowing you will write in the morning..."
— *Shelby Foote*

I hear my phone alarm vibrate softly under my pillow. On any other morning this would make me wish I had more time to rest, but not today. Today is Friday, and Fridays are different.

I slip out of bed as quietly as I can. Everyone else will sleep for at least three more hours if I can sneak out quietly enough — not an easy task when you live in a 200-square-foot home where everyone sleeps just a few feet from the door, but I try anyway.

It'll be two more hours before coffee shops open their doors, but I don't need coffee for this. It's Friday — togetherness tip writing day — and I've got three hours to make some magic happen. I settle into my favorite writing spot, open my MacBook and pick up right where I left off the night before. *How do I express something valuable and life-giving, something real and inspiring about this thing I love so much — this thing we're all looking for and working so hard to achieve — this thing called togetherness?* I wonder.

Just like every Friday, I doubt myself. I look back over the togetherness tips I've written and think, *Did I really create all of these? Do I have it in me again this week?* You, dear reader, push me on — the dream that you would find what you're looking for in my words keeps me working long after I think the magic has disappeared. It is the honor of my life that you are here, and I hope you find what you need.

I'm not an expert on family life nor am I a therapist, a psychologist, or any other type of "-ist". I've just been chasing family togetherness long enough to know that true, lasting family connection is achievable for all of us, and it starts in the everyday small stuff — right where we are this very second. I believe in the power of parenthood, the potential that lives inside of every single parent who loves a child and wants what's best for him or her. I believe that parents are the key to family togetherness and so many good outcomes for our kids — not government intervention or fancy programs, not mentors or teachers, not even schools or churches — parents. Not just the organic lunch type of parents, the extremely talented craft-making mamas, or the highly educated homeschooling experts either — plain old parents like you and me starting small, doing our best with the moments we have, and starting over every time we get it wrong. We're the ones leading the way to family togetherness.

Come on, I'll walk this way with you. It's a path I'm still on and I don't plan to step off anytime soon. It's not an all-or-nothing kind of thing. Instead, it's a do-what-works-for-you and it's-never-too-late kind of thing, and I hope this is only the beginning of our walk together.

I'm keenly aware of the mistakes I've made as a mom, the things that make me unqualified to write about family togetherness or show you the way to anything. The path of imperfection seems to be mine every single day, but just like you, one thing never leaves me — this incredible desire to love my family completely and to be completely loved by them for years to come.

I've been the frazzled mama, the forgetful mama, the too-busy, depressed, mentally absent mama; I've even been the boring mama, the self-centered mama, and the utterly preoccupied mama, too. And so many times during those moments, shifting to something better feels just beyond my reach, but again and again, I've found that even on my worst mama days, it's one little togetherness idea that turns everything around.

One little idea brings us back together. One little question breaks the disconnect. One little thing can change our entire homes and create togetherness where before there was strain, stress, or even pain.

In this book, you will find 52 of these little ideas that changed everything for my family during a year that was exceptionally tough. Through learning to live in a world without my mom, helping my husband fight cancer, having my master's thesis rejected and graduation canceled, losing the catamaran that had been our big family dream, and hitting pause on our full-time travel lifestyle, it was togetherness that kept us from falling apart this year — a togetherness that came through the small ideas you'll read about here.

I sent early versions of these togetherness tips to my email group, one every week over the course of one year, and I also posted them on the togethernessredefined.com blog to share with friends and families around the world. In this book, they've been updated and edited for you, compiled under themes and packed with extra love for the world we're living in today. It's my hope that this book will give you a way to keep ideas for togetherness right at your fingertips.

This is not a normal togetherness — it's one that goes deeper and lasts longer than we've experienced before. It's something we've been longing for our whole lives and desperately want to give our children. It's not being who everyone else thinks we should be or participating in everything everyone else does. It's doing what brings our families closer together, even if that means bucking the system and going our own way. It's a togetherness that we're redefining.

Whether you're a working mama, a single mama, a stay-at-home mama, or a mama who doesn't fit into any box you've ever seen, I hope you'll find something in these pages to let you know right away that you belong here.

I hope you mark up these pages, leave highlights on my words and notes in the margins with your own. I hope you read every page of this book and leave it on your bedside table to flip through its pages for ideas all year long.

I don't always get it right, this thing called family togetherness. Just last night I was the mom addicted to an idea who couldn't make myself close my computer, and I lost two hours that I could have spent with my little guy when he needed me. I'll never get those two hours back; they're gone forever, and the idea that I was so addicted to doesn't seem so important now. But today is a new day, and I get to have another go at it. No matter what you've been through, so do you.

Let's go after those big family dreams in your heart together!

This is **not** a normal togetherness – it's one that goes **deeper** and lasts **longer** than we've experienced before. It's something we've been **longing** for our whole lives...

it's a togetherness we're **redefining**

1

Small Beginnings

"Don't despise small beginnings; small beginnings get you ready for great things."

— *T.D. Jakes*

Isn't it funny how we all want to do epic things in life, but so often it's the starting small that trips us up?

The other day one of my boys was talking about how he wants to be an inventor when he grows up. He's been saying this for years now, and it still makes my heart skip a beat every time. So, I asked him how he could start inventing right now while he's still young. His reply came quickly, "I don't know." It's the same reply I give when I ask myself about the first steps to get to my own big goals. It's the same way I feel about becoming what I want to be when I grow up, too.

Often, we've already begun, but our beginning was so small that we didn't even notice it.

My mom always said I would write a book. She also said

she always knew I'd travel the world. Even as a little girl, I was always scrawling something in a journal and itching to go somewhere new, talk to more people, and try something fantastic. I think I drove her crazy every single day, but she loved me anyway.

In truth, she was right. I've written countless books, but if you ever found them hidden away in my myriad of journals, you'd thank me that they've never seen the light of day (nor the internet). I've also done a lot of traveling, but it didn't look anything like what she or I could have imagined way back then. I thought I was meant to be a missionary traveling to different countries, hugging babies, and inspiring millions, but as the story goes, I became a stay-at-home mom living in an Airstream travel trailer seeing national parks all over the United States with my kids after a brief stint as a nanny in Australia. Not exactly glamorous or even impacting to that many people, but extremely valuable, nonetheless.

It's no wonder, then, that whenever I picture God, I see Him smiling about my crazy plans or even chuckling about the way He knows it'll all turn out. I think He's a fan of small beginnings, and now, I am, too. Maybe you can relate. However, I wasn't such an early convert to the small beginnings train. I wanted to be somebody. I wanted to go somewhere. And the only way I've kept my sanity about all of these small beginnings is by clinging to words like these from Mother Teresa: *"If you want to change the world, go home and love your family."* How true. How humbling. How inspiring.

We do want to change the world — every single one of us — and we often get frustrated when our big dreams have such small beginnings.

We also want big, deep, lasting connection with the people we love — every single one of us — and we get frustrated when our efforts have such small beginnings there, too.

I'm starting to think my whole life is going to be just one big small beginning, and I'm actually okay with that. Isn't it true that so often it's the little things that the people we love remember and treasure most anyway? And isn't it also true that if every person on the planet went home and loved his or her family, the world would be changed entirely?

If you know anything about me, you know that I've now settled into my small beginnings and I wouldn't change a single thing about being a stay-at-home mom or making the sacrifices I've made to raise my children as a traveling family. But I also know that you may be reading these words and thinking your small beginnings are way smaller than that, too small to count.

You might be thinking that your efforts at togetherness are too small because you have a career that requires you to work outside of your home or you're too stressed, you don't know where to begin or you've already blown it. Rest assured, no matter what your current reality is, the way you're beginning to build togetherness with your family is not too small, and it's not too little too late — not at all.

In this chapter, you'll find a collection of togetherness tips about small ways we can build connection with our families — the ways we often overlook and underestimate, the ways we sometimes forget to count. And as you read them, I just bet you'll start thinking about the small ways you already build togetherness in your home and come up with a few ideas of your own, too.

They may be small beginnings, but that doesn't mean they're not important. It truly is that small beginning that makes a way for the greatest things in life.

For me, one of those greatest things is deep, lasting family togetherness, and I know it is for you, too or you wouldn't be reading these words. Let's dig into this first chapter together and find a few ways we can build togetherness with our families when we're right in the thick of it and don't know how to make time or space for the big stuff.

Let's begin together.

no matter what your current reality is, the way you're beginning to build togetherness with your family is not too small, and it's not too little too late – not at all.

Don't Underestimate What You Already Do

So often, when we think about building big family togetherness with the ones we love, our minds automatically go to the big stuff like adventurous road trips, ideal camping trips, and mind-blowing family vacations. "Now that's the way to build bigger memories and stronger connections with the ones I love," we think.

But there's one thing we forget in those moments, and it's actually really important, so hear me loud and clear:

Don't underestimate what you already do. It makes such a difference.

Do you make breakfast — even if it's toast or bowls of cereal or giving directions to kids on how to fix it themselves?

Do you wash loads of dishes or load the dishwasher or help kids with chores?

Do you plan meals, shop for groceries, tackle mountains of laundry, work full-time or part-time to buy those groceries, drive to friends' houses and activities, organize doctors' visits, save for college, homeschool or help with homework, plan family outings, make smoothies, keep your house tidy, scrub bathrooms, give snuggles at bedtime, ask about their day, or do some combination of these things day in and day out for years on end?

If you do even one of those things, you are already doing so much to connect with your family — you're showing up for them.

Showing up matters more than we know, so keep showing up, and keep doing it well.

This realization snuck up on me yesterday. I was talking with someone who was asking me about my childhood, and as I sat there telling her about the family dinners, softball trips, and college conversations that let me know my parents loved me, I immediately thought, "What will my own kids say when someone asks about their childhood 10, 20 or 30 years from now?"

What will they remember most? Will it be the road trips we took or the nights when we camped under the stars? Will it be a clean home and eating meals together, the giggles at bedtime, and how they knew they were loved because of the "normal" stuff or that one epic family vacation we took?

Honestly, I don't know what they'll remember most, but I do know that all of it matters — every single bit.

If you're someone who looks at a "normal" day and immediately feels a little guilty, thinking, "We should go do something today — something really cool — but we can't, can we? Because we have too much work, too many chores, or something else 'normal' standing in our way," I want you to stop today and breathe in the normal. Be thankful for it and know that showing up even in the normal stuff is a HUGE way to connect with the ones you love.

Take a moment.

What do you do for your family that you often underestimate? Take a moment to celebrate it right now.

Embrace the Season You're In

Have you ever wanted to do something new but had a feeling deep in your gut telling you it wasn't quite time yet? Or worse, have you ever put everything you had into going after a great big dream only to realize the timing was off and you'd have to take a few steps back?

Maybe you want to teach a class at night, but you've got babies at home who are extra needy during those hours. Maybe you feel called to go back to school but there isn't a program that fits your niche or your budget. Maybe you really want to see the world, start your own business, move to a different city or country, start traveling more, or homeschool your kids, but you know it'll take a while before the timing is right. Or maybe you go after one of those big dreams and things start going sideways quickly and you have to regroup.

Me, too. So many times.

In fact, every time I go through the waiting, the wondering, and the falling on my face, it's just as difficult as I remember from last time. I think it comes with the territory of being a big family dreamer, but that doesn't make it any easier to bear.

When we're in the thick of it, wondering what step to

**take next, the best thing we can do is to embrace the
season we're in.**

As a parent, you won't always be in the baby season, so try
to embrace it and lean into those sweet baby cuddles while
they last. As a grandparent, you won't always be in the
sticky-floor, peanut-butter-on-the-couch season, so try to
embrace it and lean into every sweet, sticky kiss. And as a
sister or aunt or friend, you won't always be in whatever
season you find yourself in right now. Things will change
before you know it, so try to embrace anything good you
can find where you sit today.

**So many huge family togetherness wins happen when
we take a deep breath and lean into the season we're in
right now.**

Trust me — I've been learning this the hard way. For years,
I struggled to live up to my full potential, to be everything I
thought I should be in all kinds of areas, and then, it felt
like God benched me for a long season, and I had a choice.
Would I struggle and try to make something happen right
then, no matter what season I and my family were in? Or
would I embrace my season, sit on that bench, and listen
for a beat? Thankfully, I chose the latter (for the most part)
and have been able to enjoy some pretty exceptional family
togetherness moments because of it.

Some of us can't help it — we seem to always want to be
the person in front of the classroom, the one on the stage,
the person out in front helping others and leading them into

something great. But for me, time and time again, especially as a wife and mom who wants to make the very best of my time with my family, I've realized that my place is to lead, inspire, and help through less celebrated ways instead.

Dr. Martin Luther King Jr. called it the drum major instinct, saying, **"If you want to be important — wonderful. If you want to be recognized — wonderful. If you want to be great — wonderful. But recognize that he who is greatest among you shall be your servant. That's a new definition of greatness."**

As family dreamers, we might be tempted to try to push things from time to time. We might want to take the helm of our family life and try to forge ahead no matter what. But if the timing isn't right, that forging ahead rarely turns out well for family togetherness (and it usually doesn't work anyway). So, the next time we notice the timing is off on a big family dream or two, what if we embrace our current season and work in a hidden place to get ready for what we hope will come next instead?

I bet we'll find a new kind of adventure waiting for us there.

Take a moment.

What season are you currently in right now? What would it look like to embrace it fully right now instead of wishing you were already in the next one?

Long, Luxurious Breakfasts

There's something magical that happens in our family when we wake up having nothing on our agenda and sit around the breakfast table for an hour or two talking, reading, and sipping coffee and cocoa together. The food is hot, everyone is relaxing and chatting away, the caffeine makes our brains fire out new ideas and questions, and we connect on a deeper level.

Because we homeschool and I work from home during the week, we try our hand at this on random days of the week, folding a few learning discussions right into breakfast, and we often realize about two hours later that we might need to change out of our pajamas and move onto something else. A friend of mine calls this morning ritual "Coffee and Books," and a few other homeschoolers dub it "Morning Time" or "Poetry Teatime." We've pulled so many great ideas from those families into our long, luxurious breakfasts over the past couple of years.

Our spin on it is that we like to include dad on the days when he's home and we don't like to homeschool on the weekends, so we just call it breakfast (that way when it happens on the weekend, the kids don't even realize they're learning anything — sneaky, I know). I don't love to cook, so we usually make Instant-pot oats or pancakes, or we just do instant grits or cereal to make it simple. A special treat is when we're staying over at a grandparent's house and they make a big breakfast, the smell of sausage, eggs, and pancakes or even something as simple as a roll of Pillsbury orange cinnamon rolls calling us together around the table.

Isn't it funny how we're always dreaming up something new, fun, or amazing, when actually, the good stuff is right there around the table with us? I want to take a few extra minutes to soak it in the next time, to slow it down and see how long it can last.

If you have busy mornings during the week and sometimes on the weekends, too, maybe you can make long, luxurious breakfasts a habit in your family just once a month with a "First Saturday Pancake Morning" or "Second Sunday Brunch" and then do it more often as it becomes something everyone loves.

If you're a mama of little tiny ones or a working mama like me, you may have to get up several hours before everyone else so that you have enough work done in order to actually enjoy the long, luxurious breakfast, but trust me — it's completely worth it.

It may not work the first time you try it, and it certainly won't work every time (we have about a 50% success rate around here), but when it does, it works like magic for building memories and relationships with your family that last a lifetime. In fact, I still want to run to my own parents' house every time I smell orange cinnamon rolls, and my boys always think of their Nana Amy when we have pancakes.

Take a moment.

What does breakfast usually look like in your house? What would happen if you surprised your family with a long, luxurious breakfast tomorrow morning? What would you need to make it happen? Take a moment to make a plan, schedule it, and watch what happens next.

Frozen Pizza Night

Do you think having frozen pizza for dinner is a survival tool or good family fun? Have you ever had one of those days when you were stretched so thin that you were doing your best just to get a frozen pizza heated up and on the table before everyone melted into a big hungry heap? I sure have — many, many times.

This used to make me feel super guilty, wondering *"How could I call that dinner? Wasn't I supposed to be cooking big, healthy meals every night? And if I couldn't manage it, wasn't I failing as a wife and mom?"*

This really hit me hard when my kids were little. By the time 5pm arrived every day, I was completely spent, and the last thing I could do was find something to occupy my little guys while the hubs and I cooked an elaborate meal in the kitchen. It just wasn't possible on most days. So we ate a lot of frozen pizza, and I added salad or raw veggies to make it at least a little healthy.

As a young mom, my life felt like a series of tiny, delicate plates precariously perched and spinning on top of a million tiny spindles and if one more thing came my way, they would all come crashing down.

I spent way too long trying to keep those plates perched and spinning, but then I started reading and hearing about the idea that balancing everything perfectly might just be a myth. I started talking to some friends, and I realized that balancing it all just wasn't actually possible. Some people are rocking beautiful family dinners some days and other things other days. Others are rocking other things like crafts or hiking or writing a book or family travel. But no one is rocking all of it all at once.

And I realized that frozen pizza nights could actually be really fun family time.

Not too much work on the front end, not many dishes to wash on the back end, and really happy kids sitting at the dinner table chatting away with their parents. So all these years later, we're still having frozen pizza nights in our family. They're our go-to on days that are just too full, and they continue to open up extra time for family fun.

I think that's why frozen pizza exists — for families who need a night here and there to have an easy dinner at home, right?

The truth is that as parents, some days we do cook really big, healthy meals for our kids, and other days we're top-notch employees or business owners who only have time to cook frozen pizza for dinner. Some days we're the best moms and dads on the planet, and other days we're stellar writers or athletes or homeschoolers, but rarely do all of those things happen all on the same day.

And that's life — big, messy, dream-chasing life.

So, if you've been spinning plates and your family togetherness factor is dipping pretty low these days, the pressure is officially off. You're hearing from someone who has been there and knows that balancing it all just perfectly is just a lie that keeps us from enjoying our big, crazy lives.

And frozen pizza nights can totally be the best thing we do for our families sometimes — especially if they open up time for family fun.

Take a moment.

What would happen in your family if you enjoyed frozen pizza nights with your family instead of feeling guilty about them? Do you think we can enjoy dinners with our families no matter what's on the table?

Stargazing

"Did you get the text about the International Space Station flying over tonight?" That's how a friend introduced my family to a whole new way to stargaze with our kids last summer.

We'd been looking at the stars with our little guys for years, but I had no idea NASA would text reminders to me about it. So my friend helped us sign up for Spot the Station (a NASA website that sends you a text on the days when the International Space Station is going to be visible at your location) and download the SkyView app to help identify constellations, planets, and the ISS when it passes over. Then, one night we all met up at the time NASA said the ISS would fly over, and guess what — it did! It was so big and bright, and we were all right there watching it together.

The kids were amazed, and we had a new fun thing to do together.

I signed up for the alerts that night, and I've been getting them for a couple of years now — telling the kids each time I get a text about what time the ISS will be passing over. Sometimes we go see it and sometimes we don't (because sometimes it's flying over at 3am), and it's been a fun addition to our stargazing nights. I have to tell you though, we don't just stargaze on the nights when the ISS alerts come. We like to stargaze whenever the mood strikes us.

We've seen the Milky Way on top of a mountain in Maine, said "hello" to Venus and Mars in the early morning sky in Florida, spotted meteors raining down in three different states, and even ventured out to a few nighttime National Park ranger events to learn about what it is we're seeing up there. But all of that started because our kids were just as amazed as we were the first time we saw so many bright shiny things in the sky on a clear, dark night.

You might be thinking that sounds too complicated for your family, but actually, the opposite is true. Stargazing is one of the simplest ways to have fun together, and the memories last a lifetime.

A warm night, a clear sky, and an area with low light pollution are all you need for a few hours of family time together looking at the stars.

You don't need to be an astronomy expert, and you don't have to give a lecture or identify all of the constellations. As multiple park rangers have told us, you can make up a story about any star formation you want and use it to impress your family or you can simply spread out a blanket, lie on your back with your kiddos, snuggle in close, and look up. They'll probably come up with their own stories like the guy we met in the Florida Keys last year who had found E.T. in the stars and brought his high-powered telescope to show it to us.

One of my favorite stargazing moments happened last

winter when we were in Florida. We were sitting outside on a dark night with the kids looking for a potential meteor shower when we saw a big white light traveling fast across the sky. We just knew it had to be the ISS, so we grabbed our phone and put on SkyView, and sure enough — it was! We had spotted it even without the text telling us where to look, so for the next several nights, we sat out there as a family long after bedtime looking up at the sky, watching for the ISS, talking and laughing and just being together.

I hope when my boys are older, they'll remember those stargazing nights and feel that same excitement and connection with us again, and I hope the same thing for your family, too.

Take a moment.

What would it take to get your family outside for a stargazing adventure when the nights are warm in your part of the world? Take a moment right now to set aside an evening or two in your calendar for stargazing nights — you'll be so glad you did!

Declare a "Be" Day

"What do you do?" It's a question I get all the time when people learn that we've been a full-time traveling family for almost 7 years now. I get it. They want to know how we make money if we're never in one place for very long. It's a valid question and I don't mind talking about it, but what I really wish they would ask instead is, Who are you? What do you love most? What makes you come alive? What kind of person are you becoming? How do you want to be remembered?

Because what I do for money is simply not who I am, and it took me way too long to realize that fact.

We all *do* a lot of things. Some of us manage or design software systems, teach school, cut and style hair, or own our own businesses, while others sell insurance, do online marketing, make jewelry, design logos, write books, help patients recover, clean houses, or manage financial records. Some of us stay at home while others work outside the home to lead meetings, run big businesses, or help nonprofits thrive. Some of us do several of those things at the same time and some do one thing for a while and then find we've taken a wrong turn and switch to something else. We all do other things, too — the not-making-money things like taking kids and relatives where they need to go, visiting people we love, making meals, cleaning our own houses, etc. And somewhere amidst all of the *doing*, we forget about the *being*.

It's easy to do because we all talk so much about our work and tend to put people in boxes based on what kind of work they do, but it's not all that often that we ask each other about our hopes and dreams, what we feel like we were put on this planet to do, and what we really enjoy. If we did, I think a lot of those boxes we put people in would disappear.

The truth is that our families don't need what we do nearly as much as they need who we are, and it's up to us to really show up as who we are, despite all that we do.

It's hard to balance the two. That's why every year around the holidays, everyone in my house takes extra time away from work and school so that we can schedule in some "Be" days. On those days, we don't do a whole lot of anything. Instead, we find time to be who we are, find something we love, and enjoy being on this planet. Inevitably, those "Be" days leave us feeling extra thankful for each other, wanting to do more together and be more together, and I come away realizing how these "Be" days are a game-changer for family togetherness.

If you happen to like to *do* a lot and struggle to take "Be" days like that girl who stares back at me in the mirror every morning, here are a few ideas that have worked for us:

- Stay in your pajamas on a rainy day and see what happens.
- Park yourself in a chair with a journal or book and

listen to the flow of your home when no one is really doing anything at all.

- Pull out an activity you don't do together very often (a board game, a deck of cards, etc.) and see how long you can linger over it together.
- Extend mealtimes by keeping the conversation going and see just how long your kids will talk and just how soothing it is to be with them without having to rush to the next thing.
- When someone asks, "What are we doing today?" let them know there's no agenda — we're just hanging out — and see where it goes from there.

My guess is that you'll find yourself doing plenty of things together that you wouldn't have thought of if you hadn't set aside time to just be.

At the end of the day, I just bet these "Be" days will stick in the minds of our families for years to come so that when people ask us to describe each other, we might just talk about who they are more than what they do.

Maybe instead of saying, "My husband is an accountant" or "My son is at the top of his class," we might be able to say, "My husband is the most creative guy I know" or "My son loves to tell funny jokes." I personally dream about people asking my kids what their mom is like, and instead of them responding with "She does computer stuff" or "She's a writer", they might just say something like, "She's the bravest, smartest, most loving and talented woman you'll ever meet. She loves to hike mountains, swim in the ocean, read books, write about our family, hang out with us, and give giant hugs and sloppy kisses." I hope they talk about the things they learned about me on a "Be" day rather than all the stuff they saw me do on the regular days.

Whatever you dream about your kids saying about you, I just bet they'll find that part of you on a "Be" day, too.

Take a moment.

What would it cost you to have a "Be" day with your family this week? Would it be worth the price? Take some time to think about how often you'd like to schedule "Be" days for your family, and then make a plan.

Turn Stuck at Home into Fun at Home

Running into Target when shelter-in-place orders were rumored felt like taking a risk, but I took it. I'm always cautious during flu season, so I thought I would be okay, but I had no idea at the time just how bad the coronavirus outbreak was going to be or just how long it would be before I would return to Target again. Thankfully, I didn't see anyone panicking or buying up all of the toilet paper and bottled water like I had seen on the news, but I did see something I'll never forget.

There was a little girl and her mom in the checkout line front of me, and they were buying a bright red party dress along with a few other non-essentials and kid treats. They were smiling at each other, clearly having a good time, and the little girl looked at me and my two tall teenage boys and said, *"That's my new party dress."*

So of course, I asked, *"Are you having a party?"*

Her mom's reply came immediately, leaving an impact on me that lingers even now: ***"Every day at home is a party for us."***

She went on to tell me about how they love to watch musicals and movies together so that her daughter can twirl around in her party dress, how they put out some snacks and make it into a party for just the two of them.

My heart was bursting. I wanted to scream out, *"You're rocking it, mama! I think I'll go home and have a regular everyday kind of party with my kids, too."* I'm pretty sure she would have thought that was bonkers though, so I just smiled a big goofy smile and stammered out something about how that was such a great idea.

But I just couldn't forget it.

In the days after that encounter, families across the United States and in many countries all over the world found ourselves stuck at home indefinitely with school transitioned to distance learning, work being done remotely, and even homeschooling families not able to get out to gatherings, libraries, and museums like we normally do, and I couldn't help but think,

What if we turned *stuck at home* into *fun at home* no matter the age of our kiddos?

That would be a family togetherness boost for sure.

So I shared this story far and wide and saw so many people doing just that - taking a scary situation and turning it into something really fun for their kids, and I did the same thing for my boys, too. And then, the shelter-in-place orders dragged on and on for weeks, and even as the restrictions started to lift, there was a possibility that we'd all be sheltering in place again if things didn't improve. Even as I write this, we're all living a new normal, poised to encounter cancelations and move everything back to shelter-in-place if need be. There are challenges, I know — challenges us homeschooling mamas know all too well about balancing work and school, life and productivity - but we can have some real fun and build deep connection whenever we're stuck at home if we look for it.

Here are our favorite ideas:

- Making something together

- Reading books aloud or listening to them on Audible

- Hiking in the backyard

- Letting the kids get bored and seeing what they come up with

- Playing board games and card games

- Closing the computers and getting outside to toss a ball

- Cleaning out old toys and books and soaking in their memories

- Declaring a "Be" day

In the surreal days and weeks that followed that first announcement about flattening the curve for coronavirus and staying safe at home to fight a pandemic, every big company, small business, blogger, writer, and leader in the world seemingly stepped up to the plate to provide free resources or extra help for everyone stuck at home. We enjoyed book lists, encouraging articles, free audiobooks, YouTube science lessons, homeschool support, game-schooling ideas, podcasts, and all kinds of fun things.

And we turned *stuck at home* into *fun at home*, wondering if and when we might have to do it again.

As I talked with my mama friends about the pandemic and how we can use quarantines, canceled events, and extra time at home to build togetherness with our families, one piece of advice tattooed itself to my soul. "Slowing down is good for everyone," she said. I bet she wouldn't have had to tell that mom in Target line that; she had already found the joy in slowing down and being at home with her little one. I hope we all find that slowing down is a togetherness boost.

Take a moment.

Take a few moments to make a list of your favorite things to do together and keep it handy for the next time you're stuck at home.

Clean Out the Toy Box

Have you ever had too many busy weeks in a row? Bored tweens and teens in the house? Have you ever felt too overwhelmed and overworked to get to do anything fun with your kids? Does it ever feel like you just can't get away from the mundane long enough to do what really matters?

No matter what's going on in our house at any given moment, I keep a little secret in my back pocket for those moments when nothing else is bringing us together. I forget about it far too often, but when I remember, it works every single time.

That secret is cleaning out the toy box together.

Not the chore kind of cleaning out — the adventure kind.

Last summer while my oldest son was away at day camp, I had some one-on-one time with my youngest, and we decided to clean out the toy box. He was going through the early tween phase where he spent so much of his free time searching for something he really loved to do and I always love a good cleaning day, so this felt like the perfect activity.

Every morning I simply got out a few of our Lego boxes and worked with him to find a flow for sorting, and then he was busy for the rest of the day with the fun things we found.

We found Lego minifigs we haven't seen in months, trinkets from when he was tiny, and some of our old favorites that have been hiding in dark corners. We even found some cool things to show his brother when he got home from camp every day.

We talked about our favorite memories with those old toys, told stories, and revived some old toy flames.

It was magic — definitely something I don't want to forget again.

Why is it that we forget things like this? Maybe it would lose its magic if we did it all the time, but just in case it won't, I'm going to try it again soon. I just love the connection it brings — especially for kids who are older and may not open the toy box everyday anymore. There's just something about the threat of losing a toy to the donate pile that makes it become suddenly fascinating, right?

An added benefit for us was that this little activity of connection and cleaning sparked an organization overhaul throughout our entire tiny home. My little guy got motivated to do some big cleaning chores to earn a new toy he's been wanting, and I got motivated to organize other out-of-control areas, too. We cleaned out the pantry and spice rack, reorganized the school closet and even cleaned out our messy truck, too.

I forgot how good it feels to have everything clean and organized — it feels really, really good.

In fact, it changed my perspective in a few unexpected ways even. Things just don't seem quite as overwhelming when I have an organized home. I ended that week feeling like I could tackle anything, and I had two kiddos with a whole pile of toys, games, and art supplies to try again.

I'd say that's a family togetherness win for sure.

Take a moment.

How long has it been since you cleaned out the toy box with your kiddos? If you're due, find a few hours in your schedule and pencil it in. You won't regret it.

Know When You Need to be Alone

Some weeks are tough for me. Every single day seems to be filled with more to-do's than I could possibly do, the kids need extra attention, my phone rings constantly, and my email inbox looks like the next set of *Hoarders*. On weeks like these, the last thing I feel like I have time for is self-care, and yet, I feel myself spiraling with no chance of digging deeper to power through.

Does this ever happen to you? Do you ever feel like you're sitting on empty and there's no gas station in sight?

On weeks like these, I know I need to be alone for at least a few minutes to recharge, but so many times, everything else gets in the way. So I just keep going and going until the overwhelm and migraines set in.

I especially know I need a course correction when my sweet teenager comes over and gently says, "Mama, how about you take a break right now? I think you need one," which happens more than I'd like to admit.

When this happened a few weeks ago, the look in his eyes said everything. It said, "I need you, Mama. Stop pushing so hard. I'm right here, and I see you." I felt like I couldn't take a break at that very moment, but I did start looking for a small window — and I found one. I grabbed my yoga mat, headphones, journal, and a quiet place, and I spent 90 minutes with myself. Afterward, I felt like myself again.

As mamas we know that time alone can't always happen, but when we're intentional and we understand that we need it, we can find it.

Here are my favorite ways to find time alone when I need to:

- Grab the earbuds and go for a walk.
- Set a timer for 30 minutes and call a house-wide "quiet time".
- Take a book outside and read under a tree.
- Hang up a hammock and pretend to nap.
- Stand outside directly in a sunbeam for 5 minutes.
- Go on a solo hike and put my phone on silent.
- Get up early and go to a coffee shop to write.

Sometimes it's hard to prioritize this, but when I'm intentional about carving out time for myself to be alone, I can tell a difference in the way I parent, the way I work, and the way I enjoy my family. (I can also tell that they enjoy me more, too.) But so often that ugly question takes over:

Is making time to be alone really that important? Shouldn't I be doing something else?

And here's the answer I come back to again and again —

If being alone for 5, 10, 60, or even 120 minutes makes us a better version of ourselves, if it recharges us and helps us gather strength, if it makes us feel healthier, it if brings ideas and anticipation for the next time we get to spend with our families, then making time to be alone is the best thing we can do — for ourselves and for our families.

Admittedly, my kids are older now, so it's a lot easier than it used to be to carve out some time for myself. Moms of little ones certainly can't just abandon ship to take a bubble bath or leave the little ones at home while she goes out for a run, but I've seen my friends in this season right now rocking some creative solutions like asking family members to cover one meal per week, starting the tradition of "Daddy Day" every other Saturday, or hiring a babysitter for just 2 hours to make solo grocery store runs.

In fact, I believe that getting alone and letting ourselves miss our kids can be one of the biggest ways to build a strong family culture of togetherness.

You just can't force these things.

Take a moment.

How do you know when you need to be alone? Have you ever felt like everything was falling apart but after just a few minutes alone realized it was just a break that you needed? Ask yourself how you might know when you need to be alone next time.

Stay Home a Little More

How does it make you feel when you think about staying home a little more? When I first wrote about this in our email group, none of us knew that COVID-19 and something called "shelter-in-place" would be in our future. No one could have predicted that staying home with closed businesses, lost jobs, and even temporarily shut libraries would go on for months, leaving many of us feeling at least a little stuck at home. But now, as I write these words today, some of the restrictions are starting to lift all over the world, and we're emerging from our homes again. I don't know if all of us will return to the level of busyness and on-the-go living we had before we heard the word *coronavirus* (and I'm not sure we want to), but I think you'll agree there's beauty in being home with our families if we look for it.

If I'm honest, I have to tell you that staying home is not often my first choice — I'd much rather go camping, hiking, road-tripping, or national park visiting. But on the long list of ways to bring our families closer together, staying home a little more can't be overlooked.

As an extrovert who loves to get out and about, I never thought I'd say this, but staying home more, whether for a day, a weekend, or as a stay-at-home mom has been a huge togetherness win for my family. I'm not alone either - I've heard from so many others who say the same. It's certainly not easy for anyone who tends to be a people pleaser or a busybody (ahem, me), but it's so worth it.

It all started for me when I became pregnant with my first son and experienced an unexpected longing to be a stay-at-home mom — an idea that wasn't popular and still can be controversial these days.

But it's something I think so many parents struggle with — this desire to be with our kids more and the pressure from society to think that's not enough.

Somewhere along the way, we learned that going to church every Sunday, showing up for everything we're invited to, and packing our family's every free moment was the way to a happy, successful, good-citizen type of life. But for many of us, it only takes a few years of trying to make that happen to realize that it just isn't sustainable, and it's not good for building a close family either (especially if you have an introvert or two in your home like I do).

So, I had to learn early on that sometimes we just have to say "No thank you" and stay home with our people. We talk, laugh, read books, play games, stargaze, and do all sorts of things, and my extrovert heart gets fed right along with their introvert ones.

When we stay home a little more, the reward we get is tremendous — inside jokes to share, memories to recall, and a lasting impression on our kids about just how much they matter.

I have to admit, though, I learned this the hard way and I'm still learning it every time I wake up with an antsy feeling and think I can make everything better with a big adventure of some kind. Thankfully, I have a few people in my house to remind me, and yes, I'll admit that having a home that can roam (an Airstream) and making our home all over the United States for the past seven years makes this little togetherness tip a whole lot easier for folks like me, but don't let that stop you from making it work for you, too.

Take a moment.

When life gets busy, how do you know when to say no to something so that you can stay home a little more? How do you find balance and reconnect? Or, if this is an area where you could use some improvement, schedule a trial run.

2

Big Dreams

Now that we're loving our small beginnings and embracing the knowledge that everyone starts small and that most of us have to start small more than once, let's talk about big dreams.

I bet you've got some big family dreams, don't you? How long has it been since you thought about them? When I ask myself these questions, I immediately want to dig out my old journals and see what I was dreaming about back in 1999, 2009, and even 2019. Can you remember your dreams with everything that's been going on lately? Do they still apply? Before we go any further in this book, let's take a few moments to write down 10 things we dreamed of when we first became an adult, first got married, first became a mom, or first heard that we'd be sharing our lives with the people in our house right now. What was the dream way back then? What are the new dreams that have emerged since then?

My guess is you might be like me — some dreams still have life in them, some are on the backburner, and at least a few are on the "no longer apply" list.

The summer after my 10th grade year, I attended a week-long youth leadership retreat on a college campus with a bunch of kids I didn't know. We learned about organizing service projects and making speeches, resisting peer pressure, and being ourselves, and we learned that we could lead ourselves into our biggest dreams in life if we were intentional about it. (I also learned that I was a terrible dancer, but that's a story for a different book.) On the very last day of the retreat, we were asked to share our biggest dream for the future with our large group, and I remember my moment like it was yesterday. Without hesitation, I stood up and boldly declared, "I'm going to be a medical missionary to Australia," taking my seat with a big smile (and probably writing the phrase in my notebook).

In the coming years I would discover that my stomach was far too queasy to even hold a tray of supplies in the medical field and that Australia needed medical missionaries about as much as America did. I would also discover that becoming a missionary in the traditional sense wasn't in the cards for me either. But one thing stuck with me about that dream statement — I would move to Australia.

And move to Australia I did, as a 25-year-old with a

husband and a toddler to happily work as a nanny while my husband attended college. We lived in a one-room garage apartment in the Sydney suburbs where we brought our second baby into the world, and as humble as our circumstances were, we were living our dream life.

Isn't it funny how big dreams can take over our hearts and minds, and even when we grow out of certain parts of them, they continue to leave their mark on our lives? It makes me think that perhaps those big dreams weren't actually our own creation after all but rather, a peek into the future with a few details missing.

What big dream has been in your heart from the time you were young that's still hanging around, morphing into a big family dream, and asking you to give it a try?

As my family's story goes, we quickly ran out of money living our dream life in Australia and hobbled back home to the States to get back on our feet again. A few years later, we started living a life of chasing a few other big family dreams we never knew we had. With a truckload of doubts and fears, we tried homeschooling our kids. With trembling hearts, we bought our first big home and then sold it to move to the coast. With shaky knees, we left our traditional lifestyle to travel full-time and see all 50 of the United States. With a pit in our stomachs, we left our land travels to live on a boat. And now, having tried all of those big dreams, we're still dreaming big and still facing the fear that comes right along with it.

Maybe you can relate?

Whether we go after our dreams or leave them to wait us out, we still have some overcoming to do if we're going to step into the kind of family life we really want. Eleanor Roosevelt said, "The danger lies in refusing to face the fear, in not daring to come to grips with it . . . You must do the thing you think you cannot do." And I wholeheartedly agree.

Maybe your big family dream is to own a family farm or move to a new city, state, or country. Maybe you want to be home more with your family, work less, have more time to play with your kids, or travel together to see things you've never seen before. Maybe you want to adopt a child, live overseas, homeschool, travel, or spend more time outdoors as a family. No matter what your big family dreams are, they can be big for family togetherness — and, hey, they're important too! In this chapter, you'll find togetherness tips to spark your desire to keep going after them. Read them as many times as you need to and make your own list as you go. I still dig these out when I find my resolve flagging from time to time, and I hope you'll find yourself doing the same.

Keep dreaming!

Whether we go
after our dreams
or leave them to
wait us out, we
still have some
overcoming to do
if we're going to
step into the
kind of family
life we really
want.

Find Your Family's Thing

Every family has a thing. Whether they call it their sweet spot, the good ol' days, or just doing what they do — it's there somewhere. Some families find their thing right away, and for others, it takes some time.

Whether it's camping, traveling, horseback riding, baseball, academics, church, soccer, music, dance, theater, homeschooling, the family business, hiking, puppies, or literature, I bet you're thinking about something right now that might just be your family's thing.

Or maybe like me, you won't decide easily. When I was newly married and my kids were really small, all of my friends were settling into their families' things — baseball, school groups, dance — but my family didn't find our thing easily.

And then one day, we realized it was okay that we were a little different and that might just be our thing.

We loved to move to different communities and meet people, settle in for a little while, and then move again. We saw ourselves as friend collectors, moving around and making friends all over the world.

But that couldn't be our family's thing . . . or could it?

As it turns out, it could — we stopped moving to different houses, moved into a little house we could take with us (an Airstream), and quickly became "that traveling family" chasing adventure in an attempt to be together more, and we've been using travel to connect as a family ever since.

It's the thing that makes us different — the biggest way we bond with each other, and while it was hard at first, these days we're really liking that it's our thing.

But full-time family travel isn't for everyone, it won't last forever for any family, and honestly, it's not something to be taken lightly. It just happens to be the thing that helped us get out of our rut, open up our minds, and meet people and have experiences we never would have otherwise. It makes our hearts sing and brings a smile to our faces. It's just our thing.

You might be wondering, though, how exactly to find your own family's thing. Here's the best way I know — you find it by looking and trying new things . . . together.

If my experience has taught me anything it's that you'll rarely find something you're not looking for, but when you look, you'll find it. And in that attempt to find the thing that most defines our families, we're having conversations with our spouses and kids we'll remember for life, we're going places together we've never been before, and we're connecting in ways we never knew possible.

Now that's togetherness if I've ever seen it — getting excited about something that we have in common and watching our family relationships grow stronger.

Take a moment.

Write down a few ideas you think might be your family's thing. What do you like to do together most? When do you feel most alive? Ask your hubby and kids what they think and see what everyone's lists have in common. Does a clear thing emerge? Are you thinking about finding a new thing?

Visit a National Park

We weren't big national park people before we started traveling full-time, but now we know that visiting national parks can be magical for family togetherness. We had never taken our kids to a national park before 2013, and we weren't even sure what they were exactly. But the first time we immersed ourselves in a national park as a family, everything changed — we were hooked, and we haven't been the same since.

In fact, we've now visited somewhere close to 40 national parks, seashores, and historic sites, but we still go back to our very first national park every summer to spend months at a time reliving those family memories. The hiking, nature walks, junior ranger programs, sightseeing, stunning vistas, cool mountain breezes, and cold ocean waves at Acadia National Park on the coast of Maine will always hold family magic for us.

We're from Georgia — a state that doesn't have the privilege of being home to one of the United States' big national parks — and we grew up thinking national parks were those big once-in-a-lifetime adventure spots people visited out West like Yellowstone or the Grand Canyon.

As it turns out, some national parks are big and many are out West, but there are so many more national historic sites, national seashores, and other national park-like centers that are smaller, closer to home, and big on family magic too. They've got activities like ranger talks, bird watching, art classes, nature walks, movies, guided hikes, kayak adventures, boat tours, and more.

In fact, while there are only 58 national parks in the US, there are over 400 nationally protected sites where you can have a family adventure that's completely national-park-like, and many other countries have something similar. In the US, you can find these by going to nps.gov/findapark.

Here's a list of the national park spots we've loved over the years:

- Acadia National Park (our favorite)
- Glacier National Park (our second favorite)
- Grand Teton National Park (also our second favorite — we have two)
- Tuzigoot National Monument
- Petrified Forest National Park
- Padre Island National Seashore
- Zion National Park
- White Sands National Monument
- Craters of the Moon National Monument
- The National Mall in Washington, D.C.
- Campobello International Park
- Mojave National Preserve
- Joshua Tree National Park
- Big Bend National Park
- Saguaro National Park
- Grand Canyon National Park
- Arches and Canyonlands
- Mt. Rushmore and the Badlands

- Yellowstone National Park
- Mesa Verde National Park
- Guadalupe Mountains National Park
- Carlsbad Caverns
- Pipe Spring National Monument

And there are so many more we haven't been to yet! There are literally so many possibilities for finding your family's favorite national park if national parks happen to be one of your family's things.

Take a moment.

Have you ever considered visiting national parks with your family? What gives you pause when you think about it? What do you think you would find if you gave it a try? If you've been dreaming about big family adventure and haven't tried visiting national parks, take a few moments to research and see what you come up with. There may just be a few big family memories waiting to be made for you there.

Make a Big Change

I can see it on someone's face when they've decided to make a big change — the feeling of fear mixed with excitement and hope all mashed up with trepidation.

I saw it in a friend's recent announcement about becoming a foster parent.

I saw it when my parents bought their dream home and when my sister made the big leap into homeschooling for as long as it took to get her kiddo back into a good groove.

I saw it in a colleague's new baby memo and in the eyes of a family I met recently who just started traveling full-time.

And last summer, I saw it every time I looked in the mirror and every time I looked into my hubby's eyes. We had made big changes before in our 15 years of marriage, but this one felt bigger somehow — a little more risky, a little more life-defining.

Last summer, we made a big change by moving our family onto a catamaran with plans to sail from Florida to the Bahamas to Maine and back to the Caribbean the following year.

We knew it was big and crazy, and it wasn't a decision we took lightly, but still, we got all kinds of questions and doubtful looks from our family and friends. Did we have any experience? Not yet. Did we realize how much money it would cost? We thought we did. Were we aware of the risks and threats? Yes. Were we afraid we'd gone just a little too far this time? Of course.

Were we confident it was the next best step for our family's new season? You bet.

We'd been dreaming about sailing and living on the water for at least a decade, and we'd been seriously weighing what it would take to make the change for the past three years, so we decided to go for it. **"We have to at least try"** became our new family motto, and we immersed ourselves in all the YouTube videos, books, and advice from sailing friends that we could find and took the plunge.

If you've ever thought about making a big change — adopting a child, changing your family's diet, moving across the country, having a baby, living in a different culture, selling everything you have to travel with your family, or something else — you know that making a big change feels insurmountable at first — even if there's nothing you want more.

If you've ever started taking those first steps, you know those butterflies in your stomach don't subside for quite a while, but there's something about going after a big dream and making a big change that can make us come alive and be a big boost for family togetherness.

As the story goes, our big change only lasted a few months as we encountered health issues and had to sell our catamaran and return to land. But we're still glad we gave it a try, still thankful for the family togetherness boost it gave us, and still convinced that making big changes is a good thing — missteps and all. My kids will never forget that time we moved onto a boat — the good parts, the bad parts, and the ugly ones too. I bet we'll all still be telling stories about those days for decades to come.

Making a big change might feel scarier for some of us than it does for others, but it helps to know that by going after our own big family dreams, we're somehow opening up possibilities for everyone else out there who has big family dreams of their own, not to mention what we're teaching our kids about being brave and breaking out of life's ruts.

I can tell you from experience that the fear fades away eventually and what emerges next is the good stuff — something new and fresh to experience together, something really big to share as a family, something we can learn together that we've never learned before — something that's big for family togetherness.

Take a moment.

When was the last time you felt out of your comfort zone? Is there a big change on your dream list? Pull out a blank sheet of paper and take a few moments to map out what it would take to go after that dream, what you might experience in the process, and how you think it would feel to make that big change. (You can even hide in your closet if you need to — I won't tell anyone.)

Take a Road Trip

Have you ever seen that movie *RV*? It's the one where the dad (Robin Williams) drags his family half-way across the country in an RV thinking it's for a business trip but realizing somewhere along the way how being on the road with his family has changed everything. Would you believe we had never seen that movie until about 3 months after we'd been traveling full-time in an RV, dragging our own kids around on life-changing road trips? It's true — and we laughed our pants off when we watched it as a family.

The other day as I was out for a walk, I saw a tire cover with a picture of a pop-up camper that said,

"Forced Family Fun"

It made me chuckle, and it reminded me of the movie *RV* and our very first road trips as a family of four. They weren't anything fancy — just day trips to the beach or the mountains mostly, but our most memorable one was a crazy two-week adventure from Georgia to Colorado for a white Christmas (a big dream for us when we came back to the States from living in Sydney where it's summer at Christmastime).

Our babies cried, we were uncomfortable, we lost our tempers, and we ate way more fast food than anyone should, but those first road trips changed us as a family — they brought us together somehow.

That's why I love seeing so many families having adventures and taking road trips — big ones, small ones, and everything in between. As I write this, road-tripping is changing, but I'm still hopeful the day will come when we'll all be able to get out for a long road trip with our families again.

Every family has their own way of doing road trips. I bet you're thinking about a few right now. Some pack enough sandwiches for an army and stop at rest stops for meals along the way. Others save up some cash to eat in restaurants they love along the way. And still others drag their homes behind them on the road and cook their meals in a campground or grocery store parking lot.

We still talk about our first road trips as a family, mostly trying to remember where we saw this or that, and as we keep taking them, my heart skips a beat every time one of my boys chimes in from the backseat with a joke we all share from a place we've been together.

Those kinds of memories are why I think family road trips are the best kind of "forced family fun" there is.

Take a moment.

When was the last time you took an old-fashioned road trip with your family? Take a few moments to think of some of the memories you shared and make a plan for your next one.

Go Hiking

Have you ever been scrolling through Instagram and seen photos of people hiking with their families in beautiful wild places and wondered how they know how to do that? It looks so dreamy (and I'm here to tell you that it is), but for those of us who didn't grow up hiking long trails in beautiful mountain places, it can seem overwhelming to think about getting our families into hiking as a hobby for the first time.

Questions like, "Where do I start? Is it safe? Is it worth the effort? How much will it cost?" swirl in our minds.

Those were the questions we had before we started hiking a few years ago, but then, we decided to start where we were with what we had, and we found one of our favorite family hobbies.

We went on our first family hike in 2014 on a hot summer day in Knoxville, Tennessee. We were stuck there waiting for an Airstream repair and the map said there was a waterfall nearby in the Great Smoky Mountains, so we set out to find it.

After an hour of trekking up a mountain trail in flip flops, we found the waterfall and then had to figure out how to get back down without falling. As we were descending, we started noticing that despite the summer heat, everyone else was wearing boots.

Then we spent the next week with sore feet realizing why.

Our second hike was a little better, but only barely. The next summer, we found ourselves close to a beautiful overlook that was only accessible by hiking trail. This time we strapped on our running shoes and started up the trail, bringing a water bottle or two along as well. Half-way up the mountain, I started to realize that tight jeans weren't the best fit for hiking and we didn't have nearly enough water, so it wasn't the most comfortable hike we've ever done. But we muddled through.

Needless to say, our first two family hikes were full of obstacles (mostly caused by our own ignorance), but surprisingly, we still had fun together. So, we bought bigger water bottles, made sure everyone had on comfortable clothes and athletic shoes, and tried it again and again that second summer.

Before long, we looked like all of the other hikers on the trail, and after our first few stunning overlook views, we were hooked.

It's not every day you find something that everyone in your family enjoys doing together, so we knew we'd found gold. We just had to figure out how to make it work, and I'm so glad we did.

Now we try to hike once or twice a week when we're close to good hiking trails, scouring the maps for the best spots, and quickly strapping on our boots and packing up our gear when the mood strikes us. It's been a big way to bond with our kids. If school is feeling too hard, we hike. If emotions are running high and we're in a funk, we hike.

If you've ever dreamed of big family fun outdoors, start where you are with what you have – even if it's just flip-flops and a tight pair of jeans.

Take a moment.

What would hiking more look like for your family? What if you chose the day of the week that tends to be the lowest, busiest, or most stressful and turned it into a family hiking day each week? How many new places would you get to see? How many new memories would you make?

Get Lost Together

"Mama, I don't think this is the right way" is something my kids have been saying since they first learned how to talk, mostly because I'm horrible with directions and navigation but also because we're always trying something new and don't know the way yet.

It used to bother me every time I would hear those words from the backseat of the car or the back of the hiking trail, and I would think, "Do I make them feel unsafe? Do they think I'm a moron? Should I have figured this out beforehand?"

"Will it scar them for life?"

But then I realized how many big family adventures have begun over the years with the words, "I think we're lost" — and I never worried about it again.

It's more than okay to get a little lost and find our way with our families; it's actually a good thing — in all sorts of ways.

One example is the way we homeschool our boys. For years, I've worked online, set aside time for my writing, and homeschooled our two boys while we travel, so that doesn't leave a lot of time for prep and planning. As a result, I'm quick to admit that I'm learning **with** my kiddos rather than trying to learn everything before them and teach it to them. As it turns out, that strategy fits our kids really well, and it's opened the door to learning more than we ever could have imagined. They love teaching me things and discovering new concepts with me, and I get so excited when the sparkle of wonder fills not just their eyes but mine, too.

Another example is how we tend to go after big dreams in our family. We hear about something or get an idea from who-knows-where and start researching it. Then, we start talking about it and making a plan, and before we know it, we're doing something we've never done before, figuring it out as we go along. That's how we started traveling full-time, how we decided to live on a boat for a while, and how we ended up moving half-way around the world and back home again. (Some of those dreams worked out better than others.)

Like me, I bet you're not "normal" or "regular." I bet nothing about you is regular. Oh, you might pretend to be normal and regular much of the time, but when you're alone dreaming about what kind of life you want to live with your family, I bet those dreams are far from regular.

I bet your dreams are extraordinary, out there, untraditional, out-of-the-box.

Ours have been pretty out-of-the-box since our first baby was born in 2005. We've had a lot of fun together over the years, and I'm convinced it's because we aren't afraid to go after big dreams and admit that we're figuring it out as we go along. Our kids know their parents get wild hairs and do really crazy things, and they know we're going to go after those things together. Sometimes this means driving way too late at night to get to the next place. Sometimes it means losing sleep for weeks planning the next adventure or packing up everything we own again and doing something new. And sometimes it literally means driving around with a dead cell phone looking for the best way back home.

We know when we're lost, and we aren't afraid to get un-lost together.

So when conventional knowledge tells you that parents should have it all together, know exactly what they're doing and where they're going at all times, and never ever let anyone believe they don't have everything figured out, you know better.

You know that boring stuff is easy to figure out, but it's the fun stuff you're still figuring out as you go — and that's what you really want.

You know that life is way too short to only do the things you've already figured out.

You know what dream I'm talking about right now, don't you? It feels scary, and that's good. I have a gigantic dream or two waking me up at all times of the night right now, and I'm convinced it's an adrenaline rush that can't come from anything else.

Take a moment.

Do you ever feel like you can't go after a big dream until you have it all figured out? Take a few minutes to write down all of the big dreams you haven't pursued because you couldn't figure out all of the steps involved. Which ones do you still want to go after?

Take a Risk on a Big Family Dream

I hear from families all the time who have great big dreams — like crazy big, turn-your-life-upside-down big dreams. Some of them say, "Someday, we really want to . . ." and others say, "I would love to do that, but I could never . . ."

And then there are the families who realize they've been saying "someday" for way too long and decide to take a risk and go for it.

I bet you already know what type of family mine is, and I'm guessing you might be right there with us or right on the brink.

Whether your family dream is to start your own farm, buy a house, adopt a baby, leave suburbia, move across the country, visit every national park in the US, spend a year in a foreign country, learn to speak a new language fluently, go to graduate school, start a family business, write a book, learn to sail, try unconventional education for your kids, start your own family band, or something completely different, you will only know if you can jump from "I could never" to "someday" to "we're going for it" if you try.

The truth is that taking big risks is hard for all of us and it always takes much longer than expected, but it's completely worth it when we get the kind of family connection that only comes through chasing big family

dreams.

When you decide to take a big risk and go after your big family dreams, there will be butterflies, sleepless nights, and feelings of complete inadequacy. But there will also be a level of bonding that only comes when you're out on a limb together, clinging to each other for dear life.

Want to know how I know?

Because my family has been out on that limb together quite a few times now. First, we moved across the world together with only five suitcases to our name. Then, we ditched traditional life altogether and moved into a camper to travel around the US full-time. And a few years later, we moved onto a catamaran with the hopes of learning to sail and traveling internationally.

Every single time, something we thought was impossible became possible with planning, prayer, a positive outlook, and a series of great big risky steps.

And every single time, we've seen each other differently and grown together in a way we could have never imagined.

But don't just take my word for it.

Do some research and find other families who have gone after big family dreams like the ones you have. To find them, look up your area of interest + "family" on Google or follow specific hashtags on Instagram. That's how we have found so many friends who share our interests, and it's also how we've made a few long-lasting friendships, too.

Take a moment.

What about you? What big dreams do you have for your family? Write down how it would feel to take a big risk on your biggest family dream. What would it feel like to get to the end of your life and realize you never got around to it?

Unplug and Go Off-Grid

Have you ever heard the term *boondocking* or *living off-grid*? If you're picturing the families who live in the wild parts of Alaska, snowed in for months at the time with their only access to civilization and groceries by four-wheel drive or airplane, you're thinking like I was just a few short years before we fell in love with a different kind of off-grid living.

I had no idea what it was or why I needed it in my life — until I tried it.

The year was 2015, and we were headed out West. After traveling full-time in the eastern US for a while, we knew we needed a reprieve from campgrounds and RV parks, so we had decked out our Airstream with solar panels and a big battery bank to escape them for weeks at a time. One camper. One family. One long stretch of secluded beach. And enough water in our tanks and solar power in the sky to meet our every need for a few weeks. That was our recipe for off-grid adventuring around the Gulf from Alabama to Texas that winter with plans to adjust before heading farther west into the real boondocking haven lands.

While we weren't exactly roughing it in our 2014 model Airstream sleeping on memory foam mattresses, showering every day and drinking pour-over coffee in the mornings, we were officially living off of the sun for all of our power needs and using only the water we could carry or refill from national park water refill stations, and we loved it.

No parking lots, no traffic, no hustle and bustle — just us and the wild.

On Padre Island National Seashore, we woke up in the mornings with the ocean waves singing to us, spent our days exploring for a while, settling into school and work wherever we could, and walking the beaches looking for shells. We ate our meals picnic-style on the beach or inside our tiny home looking at the ocean, and we spent our evenings listening to the sounds of the wind and waves. Then we headed west to Big Bend National park, the Mojave Desert, Sedona, the Grand Canyon, Zion National Park, and Joshua Tree, tucking ourselves into national forests and Bureau of Land Management spots, carrying on with life as usual with a big, beautiful backyard and plenty of room to explore, hike, and roam on our own.

We were doing it, living off-grid — and what we found was less distraction, less hurry, and more family togetherness. So, year after year, we kept going back to the wild — to boondocking, to off-grid living.

Since then, we've had several off-grid adventures, and we still love it. In fact, we love it so much that we even tried going off-grid for a few months on a boat too. If you're anything like us, you know what it feels like to be addicted to the wild — it calls to us, and we've found so many friends who feel the same way. Some call us hippies or crunchy folks, and maybe we are, but I think that's okay.

Seven years into our full-time traveling lifestyle, we're finding a groove that doesn't include off-grid living quite as often as it did in the past, but I always start thinking about it again every Christmas. In the days that fill November through January, I often get overwhelmed and find myself so ready to be done with the "Buy me! Buy me!" culture that has become the norm of the season, pushing me back to the sweet, simple dream of going off the grid. Reminding me what it's like to talk about a stick, rock, or jellyfish someone found rather than the latest video game feature they just *have* to have.

There are plenty of families enjoying a life off-grid year-round. (We've even camped with one of these families interviewed them for our podcast.) But if you're wondering why on earth anyone would choose this kind of adventure, you're not alone. I wondered the same thing for so long — until we tried it. Despite the challenges, here are the benefits we've found:

1 – The quiet
No hum of traffic. No sirens. No televisions blaring.

2 – The simplicity
No temptation to stay on the computer too long or let the kids play video games past their screen limit for the day when you're on a power budget. There's also not a whole lot of temptation to run to the store for just one more thing when that store is a few hours away.

3 – The sustainability
The planet's not losing a thing when we're living on solar energy.

4 – The family time

It feels like we become different versions of ourselves in the wild. We're more relaxed, more hopeful, more curious, more alive.

5 – The freedom

So many things to discover that can only be discovered away from civilization.

Whether you're into wilderness camping with a tent, backpacking overnight, or taking your RV into the great unknown, having the option to go off-grid might just be what you're looking for if you're in need of a big family togetherness boosting adventure.

Take a moment.

Write about your feelings when it comes to off-grid living. Have you ever tried an off-grid adventure or two? If so, how did it feel? What were your heart-soaring moments? What were the downsides? If you haven't tried it yet, what part attracts you? What do you think would be difficult?

Share a Hobby

Whether you love to read, run, swim, write, fish, play video games, sew, scuba dive, paint, sculpt, remake old furniture, walk dogs, hike, climb mountains, or something else (the list could go on forever), we all have our hobbies. Some of us pick up our favorite hobby when we have a little time on our hands or when we need something to feed our souls, while others of us seem to be addicted to them, turning our hobbies into a career or a lifestyle, making time and space for the activities we love every single day.

Whichever type of hobbyist you are, have you ever tried sharing a hobby with your whole family — or even just one or two people at a time? I'm here to tell you it can be a big boost for family togetherness.

When I was in college, my dad took up cycling, and he invited me to try it with him. He bought a couple of road bikes, practiced on his own for a while, and then somehow convinced me to train and start doing long rides with him. I loved it. I had never shared a hobby long-term with my dad before, and our relationship deepened in those days when we were training together or off on a bike trip together. We did a 36-mile ride, then a 50, and then we attempted a 100-mile trek together too. A couple of years into it, I got married and started having babies, and raising babies caused me to hang up my biking shoes. Dad kept going, though, and got my mom into it, and they had some adventures together, too. All these years later, I still think about those moments with my dad; I'll never forget them.

The task can seem daunting — right? Finding something you really enjoy doing as an entire family might not be easy in your house.

You may have to try a few things and let them fizzle, or you may have to break off into pairs for some hobbies and come together for others, but sharing a hobby with the people you share life with can be a huge way to boost togetherness in your family.

Recently, my husband and I decided to try a whole bunch of new hobbies together with our kids and turn them into a new part of our traveling lifestyle. Sailing, spearfishing, freediving, paddleboarding, snorkeling, and saltwater swimming and fishing were the new family hobbies on our collective agenda for the next season of our life. But as we started trying to enjoy them, we quickly learned that some hobbies are harder to learn than others, and maybe — just maybe — we should take them one at a time.

We also learned that some hobbies take off like wildfire and create great family experiences, while others simply don't. So, we tried them one by one for a while, and we noticed that even the small hobbies we share with our kids — hobbies like writing, gardening, and board games — can lead to big family togetherness too.

The truth is you don't have to do every single thing together (we all need our space and personal hobbies, too), but if you're searching for a way to connect with someone in your family, or a way to bring your whole family a little closer, sharing a hobby is worth a try.

If you're running low on ideas, here are a few we love:

- Nature walking
- Listening to audiobooks
- Collecting stamps, coins, etc.
- Playing board games
- Writing stories
- Photography
- Hiking
- Gardening
- Camping
- Cooking
- Drawing
- Stargazing
- Birdwatching
- Pottery
- Roadtripping
- Archery
- Playing the guitar
- Beekeeping
- Visiting national parks

Remember: Start small and go slow, and don't be afraid to try something new.

Take a moment.

Which hobbies do you enjoy that might be a good fit for your whole family? Is there a new hobby you've been wanting to try? Make a plan and make it happen. Get out there and create some memories together!

Visit a Theme Park

<u>A note before you read this tip:</u> I wrote this story and shared it with my email group just two weeks before COVID-19 appeared in America and fundamentally changed the experience of visiting theme parks for the foreseeable future. I brought it into this book of tips in hopes that we can safely return to large gatherings again one day.

My family loves making a big deal out of birthdays. Some years that means taking the day off from school and work to visit a big movie theater, hiking trail, beach, or shopping mall, and other years, it means a bigger trip — taking several days off to enjoy something the birthday boy or girl has been dreaming of for quite a while. So, when our littlest guy started talking about visiting a gigantic theme park for his birthday this year (and wouldn't stop talking about it), we started thinking.

Our first thought was, "We really aren't theme park people," and it's true — 99% of the time, we'd much rather spend time in nature than plod around manmade attractions and stand in lines all day long. But then we started to wonder . . .

What if our family could love national parks AND theme parks, nature trails AND roller coasters, beautiful beaches AND waterparks? What if we found space in our hearts for the things our kids are obsessing over right now too?

So we took off work and school for a few days, invited some friends and family to do the same, and we spent our little guy's 12th birthday braving the crowds at Star Wars: Galaxy's Edge in Orlando. It was certainly wild, loud, crazy, and at times, frustrating, to be enjoying something so big with so many other people, but that visit was a huge boost in our family togetherness factor. Here's why:

1 – A break in the routine

As helpful as routines can be, there are definite togetherness perks to setting out for a day with our families schedule-free.

2 – Loads of time standing in line together

It's amazing how many great conversations happen while standing in line for hours on end. In the moment, it seems like we're talking about nothing at all, but after the fact, we realize that those little conversations are everything.

3 – Little or no devices in the way

As someone who works online, I appreciate the natural eye contact and attention that happens with no computers around, and if we pay attention and keep our faces off of our phones too, the screen-free togetherness magic happens all day long.

4 – Working together to figure things out

Where are we going to find some food? Which ride should we try next? How much time do we have before the next show? When my kids were tiny, I felt like I had to have an answer for questions like these, but now that they're older, it's so fun to let them help decide where and when to go, what to eat, how to get there, etc.

5 – Getting caught up in the magic
Watching our kids get caught up in the magic of Harry Potter or Star Wars, Peter Pan or Toy Story is probably enough to make any parent's heart leap, but when we let ourselves get caught up in it, too, I think it's even better — for us and for them. That's the power of a good story — it gives us so much to talk about and helps us deal with our own worries, fears, and knowledge of heartbreaking things all over the world.

It's probably true that my family will never be theme park people, just like some families will never be national park people and others will never be camper people, and that's okay.

No matter what kind of family yours is or whether you ever visit a theme park, when we find space in our hearts to care about what each one of us loves, break our routine, and pay attention to each other, big togetherness wins happen over and over.

Take a moment.

Have you ever been to a theme park with your family? What do you remember most? Ask your kids what they remember most, too. Dig out some family photos and reminisce for a moment.

3

Deep Connection

"I do not want someone who stands next to me because they are lonely; I want someone who stands next to me because they cannot imagine standing next to anyone else."

— M. Burr

Have you ever found a group of friends, started a job, or joined a club or church group and felt right at home immediately — like you'd been there all your life?

Have you ever wished you could find something like that?

I have.

I was pretty good at fitting in until I started traveling. Admittedly, I was never really mainstream, and I felt left out plenty (especially as a young mom), but I usually got by okay. As soon as I became an adult and got out of my home state those first handful of times though, I was a goner. A rebel. A free thinker. Some would even say a hippie. I lost my tether to the Celeste everyone thought I was — the one I pretended to be even when I didn't know I was pretending — and I found a new tether that fit much better, the tether of deep connection with myself and my own little family. I also found a tether to other mamas building deep connection with their families, too. And what I learned from that experience is that although every single one of us longs to belong, we often forget that we already do belong in our own homes.

Our longing for belonging doesn't have to go unmet. We belong with our people — our families. We belong with our kids and husbands. And we can build deep connection with them that lasts a lifetime.

If you read that last chapter, you've probably already figured out that one of the biggest ways my family builds deep connection with each other is by exploring the outdoors together. There's something about waking up in a forest, by the ocean, or right alongside a majestic mountain view that makes us come alive in a new way. It helps us shed our pretension and preoccupation. It strips away who we're trying to be and reveals who we truly are and makes us able to bond more deeply than ever before.

Your family doesn't have to be lovers of the outdoors to build deep connection — that's just the way we do it. You might have that same feeling when you play board games together or build model cars. You might feel most alive together when you're at the baseball field or when you're redecorating your home, reading the newspaper, chatting over big family dinners, or doing something I've never even thought of!

In this chapter, you'll find togetherness tips that have helped my family build deep connection with each other — things like one-on-one coffee shop chats, campfires, homeschooling, writing notes for each other, creating new family traditions, and my favorite way to spend those 18 summers we get with our kids: camping.

No matter how your family likes to bond, I hope the ideas in this chapter give you fresh inspiration and encouragement to keep building deep connection with your family. I hope you write in the margins, underline your favorite parts, and take notes on all of the ideas that come to you as you read these pages. I'm right here with you exploring ways to build deep connection with our families together.

Let's see what we can get into.

We belong with our people – our families. We belong with our kids and husbands. And we can build deep connection with them that lasts a lifetime.

Make Birthdays a Big Deal

"I hope you're okay with birthday cake for breakfast," I said to a sweet friend who'd driven hours to stay with us for my oldest son's big third birthday bash. "Of course," she said, too polite to say anything else, but I could see the question on her face.

And then she found out our family secret: if someone in our house is having a birthday, we're having birthday cake first thing in the morning along with presents, candles, balloons — the works. Every. Single. Time. It started when I was a kid and someone gave me a t-shirt that said, "Today I'm the birthday queen."

From that moment on, I've been infatuated with birthdays, believing that if it's someone's birthday, that person should be treated like a queen or king all day long. I agonized over this when I was small, feeling powerless to make it happen for my parents and sister, even to the point of driving my parents up the wall.

So as soon as I started my own family, I knew what our first family tradition would be: big, big, big birthdays celebrated from the moment the birthday boy or girl opens his or her eyes another year older.

And boy have we had fun.

I knew it would be. After all, who doesn't love to be celebrated just for being born?

What I didn't know was how much connection it would bring for all of us.

Here's what worked for us when the kids were tiny:

- **Trips** to the aquarium, dinosaur museum, playground, zoo, mountains, snow, beach, or wherever they dreamed up (within reason) on the day of their birthday
- **Parties in the theme of their choice.** One year we had 3 themes at the same party because my 3-year-old couldn't pick, and another year we stayed up super late making a Monopoly cake and setting up 5 different types of Monopoly games for the next day's party.
- **Making candy** in the shape of Legos (or their favorite thing at the time)
- **Wrapping presents** in paper they picked out themselves
- **Balloons** all over the house first thing on birthday morning

It wasn't fancy or too expensive — **it was just asking what they wanted, listening to them, and making it happen.** The hardest part was putting my own ideas of Pinterest-worthy photos out of my mind to give them the party theme or trip they really wanted.

When they started school, we made **a rule that no one would ever have to do school on their birthday,** and that was a big present in itself.

And now that they're older and aren't into big birthday bashes, here's what we do:

- **Bigger excursions** farther away to special places like baseball games, a series of museums, or a fancy architectural site
- **Experiences** like skiing, tubing, snowball fights, pottery, glassblowing
- **Shopping trips** to spend their birthday money
- **Special meals** all week long on birthday week
- **Nice restaurants** they've always wanted to visit
- **Gifts** they don't expect but really want

And still, the hardest part is **asking what they want, listening, and doing it.** But the goal remains the same — celebrating the fact that we are so glad they were born and the world is so much better because they're in it.

Sometimes I fail. Sometimes I don't listen well enough and we choose an activity the birthday boy hates. Sometimes the bakery is closed, and we have to eat gas station doughnuts for the birthday breakfast (true story). But I believe they feel loved and celebrated even when all goes awry, and that's what's most important.

No matter what might go wrong, we're doing it together and making big memories, and that brings us closer every single time.

I bet you have your own ideas about what a big birthday looks like for the people you love, and if you're struggling to connect with someone in your family, that big birthday might be just the ticket. The friend I mentioned before now has a big family of her own, and I'm always amazed at the fun things they do for their little ones on their birthdays, stealing her ideas whenever I can.

The cool thing is that you don't even have to wait for a birthday — how exciting would it be to wake up to a "half-birthday" or a "quarter-birthday" or a "five-eighths birthday" excursion, cake, and party?

Take a moment.

Think about how you celebrate the people you love. Grab your calendar and jot down an idea or two you don't want to forget.

Homeschool

Bring up the topic of homeschooling in any size crowd and you'll get a mixed bag of reactions — from positive to painful. Over the past decade that my family has been homeschooling, I think I've heard just about all of them. Some of them have been inspiring, supportive, and encouraging, and others have been, well, dicey . . .

"Oh. Homeschooling. That's interesting." (with sarcastic tone and raised eyebrow)

"I could never do that. My children are just too smart."

"What do you use for curriculum? I'm an educator — that's why I'm asking."

"What type of training do you have?"

"How could you do that to your children? Aren't they lonely?"

"What about your career?"

and yes, even, *"I don't believe in homeschooling."*

So, I'm not trying to bring up the topic with you, dear reader, about the value of homeschooling just in case you live in one of the camps described above. If you do, that's fine — you're totally welcome here.

I won't try to convince you that homeschooling is a good thing — that debate can wage elsewhere. I just want to tell you a story about how it can be a game-changer for family togetherness.

This year on our first full day back to homeschooling after a long summer break, I found myself nervous because the kids had been complaining about it for weeks. They wanted summer to go on forever this year, and to be honest, I did, too. I was nervous about my oldest starting high school and my youngest starting middle school, and I didn't know how I could keep juggling homeschool with work, my own education, and our family travels. But I pulled myself together, did the research, mapped out this year's curriculum, set a few guiding principles, and bought new supplies.

Still, I just wasn't sure it would work again. The past 10 years of homeschooling have allowed us to have the best adventures of our lives, and still, I doubt my own abilities to make it work every single year. Why do I do that? All these years later, I have no idea, but to cope with the anxiety this year, I turned my nervousness into excitement, wrote the first-day-of-school-letter to each of my kiddos, and anxiously waited for them to wake up for our school year to begin.

Several hours later when my tween and teen finally rolled out of bed, we started day 1 of our homeschool for this year. Then, after a chat about our syllabus, we settled into our old routine — breakfast with books, read-alouds and book chats, research and writing exercises, nature walks, mad math sessions, individual work, and everything in between flowing just like it had in previous years. It was fun and hard, but that first day was a good day.

And all of a sudden, I realized how much I missed them when we weren't homeschooling.

How could that be? They've been right here beside me all summer long, filling their days with loads of outdoor play, reading, and video games with their pals. So how could I have missed them? We did plenty of stuff together this summer — trips to the park, games, swimming, hiking, campfires, a trip to New York City, volunteering at the library, and talking about all sorts of things. It felt like we'd had a summer full of family togetherness, but still, our connection while doing schoolwork together felt different.

That's when I realized there's a deep connection that happens in our family when we're learning together. I know homeschooling isn't everyone's cup of tea, but I haven't figured out how to get this connection any other way.

Not too many homeschoolers talk about this deep connection. On some level, it feels like if we talk about the magic, then the magic might just disappear.

But I know better — I know that plenty of families (homeschooling or not) have this kind of connection when they learn something new together. I know we're not alone.

I also know that I don't want this deep connection to end, even if we choose not to homeschool one day, or even when the kids grow up and move off to college. I hope there's a way for our family to learn something together for as long as this world is spinning.

Take a moment.

Have you ever dreamed about homeschooling your kiddos or are you in the midst of living that dream? If so, take a minute to write down what part of homeschooling brings the most connection to your family (or what do you imagine might happen in the days to come). Your pen might just surprise you.

One-on-Ones

"Let's go get ice cream — just me and you." Those were the words that came to mind the other day when I realized things were getting sticky with my littlest guy. He'd been playing with friends non-stop for days, and he needed a break but didn't know how to let me know.

I could see the breakdown coming, mostly because I've seen it in myself way too many times. So, I canceled the activity he'd planned with his friends and told him I needed his help with errands. Then, right between the farm stand and the grocery store, we got ice cream together — no agenda, no siblings, nothing but me and him and a couple of ice cream cones at the shop downtown.

Sitting in those chairs at the ice cream shop, we didn't have an earth-shattering conversation or a deep teaching moment — just a few minutes of togetherness and eye contact, and he knew there was no other place I'd rather be. I asked him if anything was bothering him, he said no, and that was that. Then, when the ice cream was gone, we finished up our errands and headed home.

A few minutes later, it happened when I least expected it. As the song on the radio ended on our drive home, it came out: the thing that bothers him sometimes.

I was so glad we were right there alone to talk about it together. So glad I'd made the hard call to help him take a break. So glad I'd taken one myself. And I realized that I don't do one-on-ones nearly enough with my kids, but it's something I can change.

The truth is there are loads of ways to do one-on-ones with the people we love — coffee at a coffee shop, a movie, dinner out, a quick walk around the block, a day hike, or maybe even an overnight away — whatever fits your style.

It certainly doesn't have to be big or long or fancy to bring connection, and you don't have to force it. You can head out for an ice cream cone and see what happens.

Take a moment.

Make a date with someone in your family today. Ask her to see a movie with you. Tell him you want to grab a coffee and chat. Go antiquing. Do a quick hike together. Whatever you do, make an effort to be completely and utterly present when it happens, and watch the togetherness magic begin.

Always Speak with Respect

A few weeks ago, I took my boys to a science center for a #fieldtripfriday adventure, and I had an encounter that made me want to scream — right at an elementary school teacher in front of an auditorium full of kids. Then it made me want to scream at myself for wanting to scream at her. What happened next turned out to be a huge lesson for me in building family togetherness. Here's the story . . .

The room was extremely noisy with too many kids talking and trying to find seats all at once, with only a few parents and teachers among them. A couple of the boys in one class couldn't decide where they wanted to sit, so they tried out more than a few spots. When the teacher noticed this, she barked, "Just find a spot and sit in it already! You're so annoying!" and then she proceeded to lash out at other students in a similar fashion.

That's when I wanted to scream at her and tell her more than a few things, one of which is that kids shouldn't be treated like cattle or told they're annoying.

Pretty quickly though, I realized that I probably would have been tempted to do the same thing if I were in her shoes. In honesty, there have been so many times I've had to push the family reset button because I've gone off the rails myself.

And then I wanted to scream at myself for even thinking about calling her out like that, and I also wanted to scream at myself for ever making my own kids feel as disrespected as those kids felt.

Meanwhile, my own kids were watching this scenario play out, shrinking in their seats as they heard several teachers barking orders at other kids. The program started soon thereafter, but I spent the entire time thinking about the way we talk to the people in our families and how it matters so much, wondering what my own kids would take away from this encounter. So, as soon as we got in the car afterward, I brought up the topic with them.

We talked about how parents and teachers always try to speak with respect when we talk to other people, especially kids, but we don't always get it right.

Then I told them about the time before they were born when I was a teacher in a traditional school with a classroom full of students and that my own behavior was pretty similar to the teacher we saw in the auditorium that day. I was ashamed to admit it, but it was the truth, and I told them that I hope we always speak with respect in our home, no matter what we need to say.

The truth is that even though we're a traveling homeschool family trying to find our way in the deep waters of desire-led learning and worldschooling, I have a lot of respect for teachers who work in traditional schools. (In fact, I wish so many of them would homeschool themselves so that they would teach at a coop and we could glean from their passion for science, experience in languages, and expertise in a whole host of things.) But so many times when even the best of us are under stress, we lash out and say things we really don't mean in ways that make others feel horrible, and we need a way to stop it.

I'm far from perfect when it comes to this and I often find myself apologizing for things I've said to the people I love the most. But there's one trick in this area that has made a huge difference in our home; it's RESPECT.

The best way I've found to help me keep from saying things I don't mean is to deeply respect the other person in every way — no matter how young or old that person is.

If I respect someone, I'm much less likely to treat him like cattle, barking at him like he can barely walk the right way or function as a human. If I respect someone, I'm much more likely to assume the best about her and listen in a way that makes her feel heard and valued. If I respect someone, I'm much more likely to hear his point of view without discounting it right away. And when I'm struggling to respect someone in my family, I can see it reflected in the way I treat them (and I bet they can see it, too).

Also, since the experts tell us that we humans are extremely apt to see only the behaviors we're expecting and looking for, I know that respecting the people in our homes will have benefits for years to come.

As we look for the best in the people who share our homes and inhabit our lives, we'll get the best out of them for years and years.

Take a moment.

Jot down your thoughts on how you can keep respect on the tip of your tongue with the people you love the most. Identify your pain points and triggers toward the negative and make a plan to go the other way next time.

Campfires

Spring is such a magical time of year for a lot of families I know. Everything is thawing, the sweaters are starting to be pushed to the back of the closet, the chill is falling off of everything, and everyone wants to be outside more. With the days warming up and the nights staying cool, spring is one of the best times of year in my book to grab my husband and kids and cuddle up in front of a campfire to roast marshmallows, pop some popcorn, and enjoy a nice, hot cup of tea.

If you know my family, you know that we've been on a big camping trip for the better part of the past 7 years, living in our Airstream and dipping in and out of campgrounds all over the country, but that doesn't mean we have campfires all year long. Campfires for us are special. They require time and attention. They require putting aside the to-do list, intentionally pulling up a chair, and settling in for a few hours to chat.

Most of the time, we enjoy the huge roaring campfires my husband and boys make right on our campsite, but sometimes our favorite campfires happen when we share them with other people. When we're back home in Georgia, my dad makes a mean campfire in his backyard for all the grandkids, and everyone ends up covered in marshmallows with smiles on their faces. When we're camping out in the middle of nowhere, I love it when a friendly face wanders over to chat around the fire we've built. And when we're settled down for a bit in the summers on the coast of Maine, we love to gather with our friends over one.

No matter who's around, campfires can be an automatic family togetherness win.

Whether your family likes big piles of split firewood or burning sticks and leaves, there's definitely a draw for both kids and adults who love watching the flames until we run out of firewood or pulling our chairs in close to talk while we stay warm.

Take a moment.

When was the last time you made a campfire to bring everyone together for at least a little while? Take a minute to pencil it into your calendar. Then, build the fire, sip some cocoa, and talk about whatever comes to mind. Lean in as your little one cuddles up to you under a warm blanket. Snag a kiss when you're cleaning sticky melted marshmallow from her hands. Tell a few funny stories while you listen to the fire crackle and notice his sweet laughter. Soak in the good moments and relish the fact that you're building memories right there in the warm glow.

Roam Around a Big City

Can roaming around a big city with kids be good for family togetherness? Honestly, most days it makes me nervous just thinking about roaming around a big city with my kids.

All of those horror stories on the news.

All of the energy it takes to keep up with little people on crowded streets.

All of the time it takes to plan activities that are enjoyable for everyone (and all of the whining that ensues from kids and parents alike if you don't).

And yet, when the opportunity arises for me to roam around a big city with my crew, I pretty much always say yes. I think about the way big cities have SO MANY great things to see and SO MANY opportunities for stepping out of my comfort zone and bonding with my family in new ways, and I can't resist.

I grew up in rural Georgia in what we call "the country" (as in, my-grandparents-were-my-only-neighbors-for-miles kind of country), and driving to Atlanta to shop or go to a baseball game was a rare big deal when I was a kid. In fact, when I turned 18, a big part of my college decision was based on me being able to drive through downtown Atlanta by myself for breaks. It was equal parts frightening and exhilarating, and I honestly didn't miss it a bit when I transferred to something more rural my sophomore year. But overall, to this day, I love visiting big cities.

So, when I got a call from my mother-in-law last summer asking me to bring the kids to New York City to have a few adventures with her, I said yes without a second thought.

The truth is we needed a reset anyway, and New York City seemed like as good a place as any to get it.

I had been drowning in work and graduate school projects, and I'd settled into a sad summertime routine of being on the computer almost every waking moment — trying hard, losing focus, taking a short walk to recharge, and then trying again, all the while feeling like I wasn't connecting with my kids and hubby nearly enough and I just couldn't catch a break to do it better.

(Yep, people who write about prioritizing family time don't have it all together either — we fail, we falter, we reset, and we try again, too. And that's where I've been lately.)

So, I said yes to the NYC trip, pushed really hard to make it work with my schedule, and I was determined that I was going to take advantage of the chance to reset and really plug into spending quality time the kids.

And you know what? It worked.

I declared myself on social media hiatus, vowed to only use

my phone for family sharing or work emergencies, squished my must-do computer work into the hours when the kids were sleeping or resting, and shut down everything for the rest of the day to spend time exploring with the kids. Pretty quickly, I felt like myself again for the first time in a long time — just me, my kiddos, and their Nana painting the town.

We ate the best food.
We watched the best shows.
We saw the best art and architecture (even Van Gogh, Monet, and Picasso).
We walked until our feet hurt.
We took a ferry at sunset to see Lady Liberty.
We biked around Central Park and played chess there like they do in the movies.
We got lost daily and let the kids navigate.
We let the kids choose the food, the activities, and even the desserts.
We took trains, taxis, and rental bikes.

We did it all.

And now that we're back home, do you know what I remember most?

I remember the way my boys grabbed my hand when we crossed busy streets and how their eyes lit up when they saw something they really liked — the Nintendo store, Strand Books, Lady Liberty, the Guggenheim.

I remember the way they laughed at me when I went ga-ga

over the *New York Times* building and Van Gogh's self-portrait and how much they enjoyed *Aladdin* on Broadway and *Stomp* at the Orpheum.

I remember how often I said to them, "I really want to take you to this cool thing on the map, but I'm nervous about figuring out the bike rentals or subway schedule to get there," and how my oldest grabbed my phone one morning and said, "Hey, I figured out how the CitiBike thing works. Let me show you."

I remember talking about the art we saw, admitting to the kids that I have no idea what any of it really means, and showing them that I'm not afraid to admit when I don't know something.

I remember how proud they were when they remembered a fact from history or mythology I had long forgotten, and how easily they stepped into the teacher role when I let them know I was totally okay with it.

I remember how they bubbled over with story after story for days when we finally got home to see their dad, and the big hugs we gave to show him how much we all missed him when we were away.

I remember the way they looked at me, and the way I was truly present to look back.

And that is something I'll never forget. It's something I've decided I need to have more of in my every day — even if I have to move heaven and earth to get it.

That's how roaming around a big city turned into a way for our family to connect on a new level and bond in ways I dream about. It certainly doesn't always happen that way, but I'm so thankful it did this time.

Take a moment.

Think about the last time you roamed around a big city with your family. How did it turn out? Was it a big family togetherness boost or an exercise in controlling tempers and growing patience? What do you think makes the difference for your crew?

Camping

It's almost here — that time of year when the madness slows down and the swimsuits come out.

Summer. No schedule. No school. No running here and there. **Sweet, sweet summer.**

Those of us who are lucky know that we get about 18 of them with our kids before they go off to college and into the world on their own.

When my kids were little, it seemed like summers with them would last forever, and yet now that they're teenagers, I feel like those 18 summers are slipping by way too fast.

"How did I get here so fast?" I wonder, **"And how can I make the most of every childhood summer they have left?"**

For my family, there's really only one answer.

Camping. It really is my favorite way to spend those 18 summers.

Camping trips can be pure magic for quality family time. It looks so relaxing on Instagram, doesn't it? The s'mores, campfires, and beautiful views. The idea of hiking all day surrounded by the most gorgeous scenery only to come back and relax by a fire all evening with your family.

But is it actually that good?

After camping with my boys all summer long for the past 6 summers, I can tell you that sometimes it is actually that good — but sometimes it's not.

Sometimes you might take a couple of weeks off from work, spend good money on a campground reservation, and spend night after night cooped up in a soggy tent.

Sometimes you might drive 6 hours from home to camp in a gorgeous spot and realize after arriving that you left your tent poles at home. Or you buy an RV and realize that everything needs repairing on your first trip out.

But other times, you get week after week of gorgeous weather, plenty of time outdoors with your family, and heaps of family memories you'll talk about for years to come.

The campfires glow every single night, the trails are perfect, the fish bite every single day, and you make loads of new camp-loving friends to sweeten the experience.

It's those good times that keep my crew coming back to a summer full of camping year after year.

You might be saying, "But I'm not the camping type!

I've never even been camping!"

That's what I thought, too, until I tried it.

I didn't grow up camping. My mom really wasn't the wilderness-loving type, and I was right there with her. In fact, when we went on the rare camping trips with our youth group in my teenage years, she and I were the first two to ditch the wet tent and sleep in the car or head to a hotel.

But as I got older, I realized that tent camping isn't the only option. Actually, there are heaps of different options for camping, and not every option is right for every family. So now I know that if my mom and I had been in a drier climate, we probably would've been just fine in that tent. Or, if we had been glamping in a fancy camper, we would have been even better. It all depends on knowing where you're going and what you need for the type of camping you'll be doing.

My husband and I started camping with our boys when they were tiny, and we always went out in a tent because that's the most cost-effective way to do it. Then, when we decided we wanted to travel full-time, we moved into a camper — first a gigantic 5th wheel and then a smaller Airstream. We've met loads of camp-loving families and seen them camp in pop-ups, tents, and all sorts of contraptions, many of them coming back to the same campground year after year with the same friends and even their kids long after they've entered adulthood. There are so many ways to do it.

And with all of our camping experience, I wholeheartedly believe that camping trips are magic for family bonding. **I'm even starting to believe that camping might be something we do with our grandkids one day, too.**

Take a moment.

Think about whether camping is something your family might love. Rent a camper for the weekend to give it a try or pitch a tent in your backyard first. With campfires, hammocks, s'mores, tramps through the woods — the whole shebang — I'll bet you'll love it.

A Little Bit of Boredom

When school is officially out for the summer each year, I immediately start thinking it's time for great big family summer adventures — adventures so magical I can hardly stand it. Every single summer day should be filled with great big adventures, right?

Not right. The reality is that while we may have a few great big adventures planned during the summer, many days don't feel adventurous at all. The reality is that most summer days are just normal. Some are even filled with big projects at work, errands that have to be run, and life that gets in the way.

Last summer, my kids spent most of their days reading library books, piddling with a few projects, doing a bit of summer learning, and playing with their friends for a couple of hours before watching a movie or playing a video game and hopping into bed. And then waking up to do it all over again the next day.

They're pretty chill about it, but there's always a nagging voice in the back of my mind wondering if it's really good for them to have nothing to do.

Should we be planning something for our kids to do all day everyday summer, spring, winter, and fall?

Then the inquiring neighbor asks what they do all day, and the mom next door talks about her kids' summer camp schedule, summer jobs, and general rush here and there, and I feel a whole new pile of mom-guilt coming on. I wonder if I'm doing right by my kids by giving them so much free time to roam around the woods, ride their bikes endlessly, and read without limits.

I wonder if it's okay for them to be bored. Will it make them more creative or ruin them for life?

By now we all know that a little bit of downtime is essential for proper brain development and learning. We know that breaks are important to recharge and get ready for more learning next year. We know that there's at least some research out there that talks about boredom being good for kids, but if you're anything like me, you still need a good kick in the pants sometimes.

Despite what I've heard, I want to know that moments of boredom are more than okay for my kids. I want to know what it's doing for them.

So, I dug into a few articles and found that

- Boredom makes kids more interesting, more motivated, and brings them meaning. - Motherly
- Unstructured, unplugged time helps kids become their best selves. - *Aha! Parenting*
- Boredom teaches kids self-sufficiency. – The *New York Times*
- Multiple studies show boosted creativity in people dealing with boredom. -*Harvard Business Review*

- Boredom can help us bring positive change for ourselves. - *Psychology Today*

And then I was able to breathe easier and let them create their own adventure on those long summer days, and what I found was a blessing in disguise — my kids doing things I never would have thought of (building forts in the woods, hunting for lost treasure in the rocks, creating potions from various elements of nature) and a mama with extra time to read her book, take a nap in the hammock, and give a ready hug, smile, and snack when they returned from their own adventures.

Now when I see one of my kids without something to do, I pause before offering a suggestion or assigning an activity or chore because I can see the magic that's about to happen. They look at me and see me smiling, and I think they can see it, too. That moment of connection — me smiling and them smiling back, me smiling and them knowing that I trust them and believe in them and know they can solve their own problems — that's the kind of family togetherness I'm looking for.

Take a moment.

Write about your own feelings when it comes to your kids being bored. How does it make you feel when you see your little one staring off into space with nothing to do for a few minutes — antsy, guilty, or something else? Does knowing the research help ease your worries? What might you be afraid of?

Shut Down the Devices

Screens — we have a love/hate relationship with them, don't we?

With our TVs, we watch movies and series and baking shows snuggled up with our families. With our consoles, we make space for video game fun for our kids. With our computers, we create masterpieces, solve problems, and change the world. With our phones, we chat with friends and family and make connections with people we've never met before on social media. We do it all — almost every single day, all day long.

We try to have screen time limits, but we push those limits right up to the edge. There seems to be so much good out there to learn and do on screens, and so much bonding to be had around them too, so we plug in more than we unplug. We relax the limits in the summer for late night movies and video games with friends on rainy days and push the limits aside completely for date nights.

Then, when things get hard or busy or uncomfortable, we find ourselves trying to find comfort from screens, but it never works.

Every family has hard days or weeks or months, and a few nights ago, my family realized we were having a big one. The growth spurts, life changes, big projects, bad weather bummers, and switching to a summer schedule finally got to us all, and we were starting to feel disconnected, crabby, and out of sorts all over the place.

I knew something had to give. So, when I finally reached my breaking point and realized nothing was helping, I declared all devices shut down for the day. I canceled work projects, shut down the phones, and let the boys know there would be no video games, movies, or tv shows that night either. They were disappointed and it took a while to convince them that they weren't being punished, but after bickering all day, they knew something had to change, too.

Later that evening, I thought everyone would quietly read in bed while I caught up the work I had canceled, so I opened the Macbook and dove into a project.

A few minutes later, my teenager plopped onto my bed with tears in his eyes, and I had a choice to make: Do I shut down the computer and lean in or give him a quick hug and tell him I'll be ready to talk in just a few minutes?

What happened next is something I'll never forget. I closed the computer and put it away to signal that I was all his, and after rambling on for a few minutes about nothing in particular, he squeezed me into the biggest, warmest bear hug for a long, long time. As it turns out, he just needed a hug and some attention from me — nothing serious, no big problems or anything — just me. In that moment, I was so thankful there weren't any screens drowning out the connection.

I almost missed it — I almost didn't put down the computer right away. I almost left it open right beside me, so I didn't lose my train of thought.

But I'm so glad I closed it — that train of thought probably wasn't worth keeping anyway.

The truth is this is hard for some families.

I get that. We were there, too, when my kids were really small. We had made a habit of putting the TV on for hours in the mornings and evenings, but one day I decided we just needed a big break from it. So we started shutting it off more and more, and eventually, we were only using it when we wanted to watch something specific.

Turning off the screens wasn't easy for the kids when they were tiny, but it got easier and easier — and we got closer and closer in the process.

And now they're totally used to asking, **"Can we watch a movie?"** or **"How much screen time can we have today?"** instead of flipping on the television willy-nilly. And they're also used to me saying **"We're not doing screens today"** when I feel like we need a break.

It's still hard on crazy-busy days when I need the kids to be distracted while I pull off a big project, but when we use screens sparingly and shut them down often, our family togetherness factor grows in leaps and bounds. If setting healthy screen limits is difficult for your family, you're not alone. I found so many stellar articles and resources on the topic, especially at iMom.com.

I'll be the first to admit that I've wanted to turn on Netflix a little too much lately to help me ignore the 10,000 things I needed to do or talk about or try to fix in the evenings with my family. And some nights that's what I do, but on those nights when I resisted and shut down the devices to lean in instead, that's when deep connection happens.

Take a moment.

Write down your ideal family screen limits. What stops you from having those with your family? Ask your kids and husband to make the same list and compare them. You might not be as far apart as you think. Or if you are, brainstorm a few ways together to come to middle ground and don't be afraid to pull the plugs and shut them down when you need to.

Write a Little Note

I have to admit something: I'm not good at writing little notes to the people I love, but when I do it, it turns the tide toward togetherness every single time.

Despite all the practice I got back in high school writing hundreds of notes to this really cute guy I met at a little country church (who now happens to be my husband all these years later), I struggle to settle down enough these days to write a really thoughtful note to the people I love.

Somehow all my words seem trite, and I find it difficult to express how I really feel.

"Maybe I'll just send a text instead, or a giffy — those are funny, right?" I think. But that doesn't always mean quite as much as a hand-written note, and sometimes I think my own generation could still learn a few things from our parents and grandparents in this way.

From the time I was young until the very last day of her life, my mom was surrounded by little love notes from my dad. They popped up on her mirror, coffee pot, and bedside table. I'm pretty sure I even saw some in her purse and Bible every now and then too. His "I love you" on a Post-It never got old to her. She wrote her fair share of notes as well, sending cards and letters to my sister and me on special occasions and for no reason at all, especially as we got older and moved away. And now that she's gone, those notes are some of my most treasured memories of her.

One of my favorite notes from my mom is the one she stuffed inside my coat pocket one morning just a few years before she got sick. I'd called her on my way from Florida to Atlanta, telling her how I had just realized it was going to be freezing in Atlanta that day, but I had misplaced my only decent coat. She quickly remembered that I had stuffed a black coat in her closet a year prior and said she would send it to me via my dad, who was just about to walk out the door to work and would cross my path if he left right away. In just three little minutes, holding a phone to her ear at the same time, my mom wrote the most beautiful little note to me and tucked it in the pocket of that coat. With "I love you so much" on the front and a Bible verse scrawled on the back, that note made me smile, laugh, and ugly cry all at the same time when I reached my hand into the pocket later that day.

That coat is long lost now (again), but I still have her note and I take it out and read it on the days when I miss her most, smiling at how much my Mom really did love me.

I try to keep this up with my family as much as I can. Surprisingly, I saw a similar smile on one of my kiddos this past Valentine's Day when I wrote a few last-minute love rhymes for a scavenger hunt. He wouldn't let me throw away those clues for quite a while, and I might have even caught him reading them when no one was looking a time or two, which made me smile all kinds of goofy smiles myself. As I sit here writing to you this morning, I'm remembering just how many times my cold, bitter heart has melted with a quick "I'm so sorry" or a longer "I love you so much" note from my husband, and I'm pretty sure he can remember a few times my notes have melted his bitter heart, too.

So, even though I'm bad at it, I know the power my pencil holds, and I try to write little notes for the people I love every now and then, especially when things get busy or weird or wonky — or even for no reason at all.

Here are a few of my go-to wins:

- Short "I love you" notes left under pillows when I leave town
- Half-page notes about big dreams on the first day of school
- Lengthy "I'm sorry" and "I believe in you" notes when I mess up
- Tiny "I miss you" notes in notebooks when I'm not there on a school day
- A simple "Have fun" written on a sandwich bag in a camp lunch
- Quick "You're so funny" or "You're the smartest" post-it notes left in a book when my kids are way too cool for the cute stuff

Take a moment.

Write a love note to someone in your family today. Make it sweeter than you ever thought you could and see what happens next.

Create a New Family Tradition

Most of the time my ideas for building togetherness with my family are pretty normal, but other times I'll throw out an idea to my husband or kids, and they'll just stare back at me like I've lost my mind. One of my most recent hairbrained ideas for beefing up our family togetherness was to start raising bees and harvesting honey together.

Admittedly, this idea wouldn't be so harebrained for many families (and would probably be amazing for some outdoorsy types), but it's something that would be pretty challenging for full-time travelers like us.

Can you imagine those poor bees living on the bumper of our Airstream while we travel across the country? Probably not, but for some reason, I could.

It was probably my serious raw honey addiction or my beautiful friend with a bee agriculture business that gave me the idea, but wherever it came from, I started dreaming about a daily family ritual of beekeeping and quickly found myself thinking that having a few bee boxes was just what my family needed to **really** get our togetherness mojo back.

Have you ever thought you'd found the thing — the one thing that would make your family closer?

Thankfully, I have a husband who keeps my crazy ideas somewhat under control. Raising bees would probably mean the opposite of family togetherness for us in this season, so I had to let that dream go — for now, at least. (It's not the first thing I've had to let go.)

And every time I let a family dream go, I wonder, "Can we still have a deep connection as a family without that one thing?"

The answer, as it turns out, is yes. Thankfully, my family hasn't fallen apart without being able to raise bees and harvest our own honey. We've also been able to build togetherness without doing a lot of my other ideas, too.

But there's something I think every family needs to build lasting togetherness — family traditions.

The old ones, the new ones, and the experimental ones, too.

I bet you might share a few of these oldie goldies with us:

- Saturday morning cartoons and long breakfasts
- Hot cocoa on crisp, fall mornings
- Bedtime stories
- 4th of July fireworks
- Family movie nights
- Back-to-school shopping trips
- Trick-or-treating with the cousins on Halloween
- New pajamas on Christmas Eve
- Turkey and dressing at Thanksgiving

- Chex mix, cheese balls, and sausage balls at Christmas

I hope these are the family traditions our kids will remember with a smile on their faces when they start their own families.

I actually didn't realize just how important those traditions were until I interviewed another mom on a recent podcast who creates small family traditions all year long. After hearing her story, I started realizing that most families have lots of daily or weekly traditions that we may not even recognize.

Here are a few new family traditions my family is trying to build:

- Sunset paddles on Friday nights
- Screen-free Mondays
- Fieldtrip Fridays
- One on ones at the ice cream or coffee shop
- Date nights
- Long hikes when persistent bad moods strike
- Campfires and s'mores

I bet you have at least a few, too.

Take a moment.

Jot down your favorite family traditions. Are there a few new ones you'd like to throw into the mix?

Stop Long Enough to Enjoy the Moment

Recently I took a mandatory two-day mental health break from everything — from work, from homeschool, from cooking dinner, from every single thing. My brain was overloaded and too tired to think, to plan, to do even one more thing. I was overextended and I knew it, so I forced myself to say no to everything for a few days, called in sick to work, and declared a mandatory fast from all business and busyness.

No writing, no computers, no cooking, no cleaning, no planning — just being.

I knew I wasn't feeling like myself, and it felt like I could either rest in a big way now or start feeling my body experience something far worse than mental fatigue later. So, I chose to rest.

On the first evening of this mental breakdown prevention hiatus, I stood on a friend's balcony and caught a glimpse of my littlest guy collecting armfuls of pinecones below and tossing them into the forest one by one, pretending they were grenades on a battlefield. I stopped to smile at him and let him know I loved what he was doing, but he was oblivious to my presence. Pretty quickly, as I stood there on that balcony, my old habits kicked in, calling me to run through my mental to-do list, thinking I should use the spare moment to preview the next day's agenda.

Then I caught myself doing instead of being and wondered, "Why shouldn't I take just a minute to clear my mind and watch my baby boy play? Isn't the over-thinking and filling every waking moment the very reason I had to take this mental health break in the first place? How will I remember him as he is right now if I don't stop to soak these moments in?"

So I let my mind find stillness and watched him, soaking in a deep sense of gratitude for more than a few minutes.

In that moment, I smiled for me, my heart grew a few sizes bigger, and I felt more love for my whole family than I had in weeks. In that one moment, I changed somehow — I got to know a side of my little boy I often rush past, and I immediately wanted more.

That moment helped me take joy in my family, and I promised myself that I would stop more often and start looking for moments like these daily.

Since then, I've found so many more family moments tucked away, waiting for me to enjoy them as often as I would quiet my mind and look for them. Some have been easy to stop and enjoy, others have been a bit of a stretch, and many I've missed altogether because I've been sending just one more text or answering just one more email.

I know we can't catch them all, but each time I grab hold of a moment and stop to enjoy it, I'm changed a little more. And I know it makes a difference my family can see.

Take a moment.

Think about the last time you stopped everything to enjoy being with your family. Pick up a pen and write about it. Or, if you can't recall the details, tuck a pen and notebook in your purse and look for a moment today. I bet you'll find one.

A Hug Every Day

The hug. Do you ever wonder who invented it? Why did it become a thing? When did humans first decide to put their arms around each other to draw another person near? I'm not sure, but I'm so glad we have it because hugs can be huge for family togetherness — even for the most bristly relative or teenager.

I'll explain.

I've been searching my memory bank this week trying to remember a hug moment that really stands out in my mind. I certainly remember the hug I gave my soon-to-be husband right after he proposed, the last few hugs my mom was able to give me before she left this earth, and the first embrace I gave each of my two little baby boys soon after they came into this world. I also remember lots more, too — the super tight squeeze from a relative or an old friend after being apart so long, the sweet cuddles of little people I love so much, and the warm embrace of a wise older friend who can always tell when I need it most.

Honestly, though, the hugs that come to mind most for me are the ones that happen in my house every day.

These hugs aren't anything out of the ordinary; they're not filled with tears or full of anything but love, but they mean everything to me.

In our house, we have a habit of hugging one another when each of us wakes up. It's something I came up with when my oldest turned 3 and decided he didn't want to be a cuddly little guy anymore. How a 3-year-old could decide that, I have no idea, but after being the cuddliest baby and toddler, he declared he just wasn't into cuddles anymore.

But I knew hugs were important way back then, and I wasn't about to let my mama days slip by without that connection. So, I created the morning cuddle. Every morning when each of us sees the other for the first time, we give each other a morning cuddle. Some days it's just a quick squeeze for my husband who barely has time before he's off to his next project. Most days it's something I have to remind my teenager to do because he's got his nose in a book he'd much rather cuddle than his mama. But every day we hug each other in the morning, and I know it matters.

A hug says, "I see you," and it creates a habit you can draw on when things go off the rails.

Every morning when we close our books and computers and put down our phones to say "good morning" with a hug, it tells them they're important. And when you build a habit of hugging every day, it seems a bit easier to offer a hug when someone gets hurt by a friend, when you need to say you're sorry, when you get bad news, or when someone wakes up on the wrong side of the bed for a day or a week or a month. These days, even my non-cuddly teenager will offer hugs when people are hurting, and they mean the world to me.

By now it's something I don't even have to think about —
when I see my hubby and kids for the first time in the
morning, they know I'm going to get my morning cuddle,
and I even try to sneak in another one at night, too. So, that
means that in 15 years of marriage, I've likely hugged my
husband at least 5,475 times. If we're married for 50 years,
I'm likely to hug him at least 18,250 times. And if both of
my kiddos are 18 when they head off to college, I'll get to
hug them at least 6,570 times (or 13,140 times if I snag a
hug at night, too) and then so many more when they come
back home on the weekends. (They will come home on the
weekends, right?!)

**Now that's a big deal for togetherness if I've ever seen
one.**

Maybe it looks different in your house. Maybe you're
better about offering a hug than I am, so you don't need to
have a certain time of the day set aside for the family hugs.
Or maybe you'd like to build a habit of hugging, but it
seems too late now.

It's not too late — it's never too late. Every habit is built
one day at a time, and if you're reading this email, you
have a day right now, so you've got all you need to get
started.

Does it really matter though?

I could share some research with you that shows how much
hugs matter for us humans or I could keep writing for a few

more pages to try to convince you, but instead, I'll leave you with a true short story.

A few years back, I had a coworker who gave the most sincere, loving hugs. I only saw her about once a month, and I didn't work closely with her on very many things. But every single time she saw me, she would give me the biggest, warmest hug and compliment me about something — my hair, my shoes, my lotion, anything. One time I got a little frustrated with her in an email exchange, but I didn't fly off the handle because I knew we had a connection and I would miss her hug if I made her mad about something as trivial as whatever was happening in our email. So, I gave her grace instead.

The next time she saw me, she hugged me tight and even told me how much she loved my hugs and how much they meant to her. One morning a few months later, I got an email from our CEO informing us that this vibrant young mother of 3 who gave the best hugs had unexpectedly passed away in her sleep. I read the email 5 or 6 times before the truth sank in. She was only in her 40s — how could she be gone like that? And how would work feel without her hugs?

It didn't feel the same, and it still doesn't. Her hugs made a difference, and as it turns out, there were many coworkers who felt the same way. She didn't just hug me — she hugged a lot of people. She was really good at connecting with people and had a knack for hugging people who really needed it. Who knew?

The truth is that our family members may never tell us how much our hugs mean to them. They may not ever even realize it themselves until we're walking into heaven one day and they're missing us. But they matter. If a monthly hug from a work acquaintance matters as much as what I've just described, those daily hugs in your house matter exponentially more. I promise.

Take a moment.

Can you recall the last time you hugged your husband and kids. How often does it happen for you? Is it something you'd like to do more? If so, don't be afraid to use the alarm feature on your phone to remind you. Some would say that takes all of the fun out of it, but I say it doesn't. Some of us have so much rolling around in our brains that it takes extra reminders to help us lean into the most important things.

Find a Date Night That Works for You

I hated date nights for 15 years until one day, I heard something that changed everything. It was Valentine's Day 2019 — our 15th wedding anniversary — and we were celebrating by spending a week in our friend's gorgeous condo right on the ocean in Oregon. Up until that point, I had always hated the idea of date nights. While I've always loved spending time alone with my husband — heading out for a hike, going out to dinner, staying in to watch a movie, or whatever else we came up with — I never got on board with the idea that we should do things like that alone together on a weekly basis.

For some reason, during the first 15 years of our marriage, while we were having babies and investing all of our time and energy trying to see the world with them, I discounted date nights as something that just wasn't possible for us. After all, if you've ever moved or traveled extensively you know that when you don't live close to family and trusted friends, you probably don't have readily available babysitters nearby, so I didn't even try to make regular date nights a priority.

Also, I really like being around my kids, especially in our downtime, so the idea of shipping them off to hang out with someone else once a week didn't seem fun to me.

As a result, regular date nights were never in the picture for us, and somehow I started seeing them as fabricated special evenings where we were forced to ignore our children for hours on end or leave them with someone else so that we could eat expensive food and watch terrible movies in stuffy clothes once a week whether we wanted to or not. (I'm exaggerating here — that's what the mind does on sore spots.)

But that Valentine's night, I heard something that changed my mind — a sound that has resulted in me making date night a priority nearly every Friday night since then.

That night I heard my kids laughing, singing, dancing, running through the house, and having the best time together, and immediately, I knew this was something they needed more of.

More space.

More responsibility and independence.

More time with each other.

More permission to enjoy some time without their parents.

And it's a good thing because now that they're older, we parents are finding that we need each other more than ever, too.

That was the first of many date nights for us, and it feels so good to say that finally, after all these years, we've been able to settle into a date night routine that really works for us. That means Friday nights are sacred in our house and we all get excited for them because the kids know they're going to get extra video game time or time out with their friends, and we parents know we're going to get to do whatever we want alone together.

Sometimes we go out for a hike or a fancy meal and let the boys do their own thing, and sometimes we just hang in our space and let the boys hang in theirs. But no matter what we do, we've got a date night routine that works for us, and it's been divine — a real boost to our family togetherness factor.

Looking back, I often wonder if we should have done it sooner, but deep down I know this:

No matter what kind of date night routine someone else says you should or shouldn't have, you have to find the kind of date night that works for you and your whole family, even if it takes a decade or more.

If you have babies right now, I want you to know that it's okay to embrace the season you're in and get caught up in your kiddos, get creative for date nights, or put them on hold for a while. You don't have to go out or leave your baby with someone else to have a good time with your hubby, but you certainly can if you're lucky enough to have a loving grandparent or friend close by. Find a date night that works for you, your hubby, and your little ones, too.

Or, if you have special circumstances, kids with specific needs, financial valleys, or something else going on right now that's drawing you to stay home a little more these days, I want you to know that's okay, too (and even good sometimes). A date night that works for you might be cooking with your hubby and listening to good music while the kids build Legos or watch a movie for an hour or two, or it might be sharing a fancy coffee at the dining room table together and chatting while the kids read or play quietly with strict orders not to interrupt. Or let's be honest, it could be an early bedtime for the kids so that you can watch Netflix and eat popcorn in bed with your favorite Netflix partner (we might have tried that one more than a few times this year).

These days, I'm writing almost every night of the week because I've got a few big projects in the works, but there's one night of the week you won't find me doing anything on my Macbook at all: date night.

Take a moment.

Jot down the ideas that came to mind when I mentioned date night early on in this tip. If you don't have a standing date night, text your hubby right now and get on his calendar — even if it's just for Netflix and popcorn.

4

For the Long Haul

"Desire waxes and wanes, and affection can be felt without long-standing commitment. But 'You matter to me' means that the long haul is accepted, even willingly taken on..."
— *Nina Sankovitch*

When my boys were little, it felt like they would be small forever. They were born just two and a half years apart in two different countries, but our home was filled with baby and little kid stuff for what seemed like forever. Then, one day, there were no baby things, the little kid toys had been donated, and that old Folgers commercial where Peter comes home for Christmas made me cry great big alligator tears. Things were changing.

Pretty soon, college plans started creeping into our conversations, our trips to the library included a peek into the young adult section, and I knew I wasn't the mama of little boys anymore; I was suddenly raising young men. My very next thought was, "I hope they still want to come home for Christmas. I hope their wives think I'm cool. I hope they bring their kids over a lot."

I tend to wax dramatic, but it has made me wonder: How do we build relationships with our kids in this season that will make them look forward to coming home when they're older? How do we show them they were made to fly but that the nest will always be a warm place they can come back to when they want to see a friendly face?

I don't want my kids to need me for every little thing when they're grown or feel like they can't live their own lives and go after their own dreams without thinking of me; I just want our bond to last for the long haul. I want them to feel like they can succeed out there and come home for a visit, too.

Maybe you can relate?

I'm not aiming to be the coolest mom in the country, and I don't have dreams of suddenly waking up as Lorelai Gilmore and having my kiddos hang on my every word. (Although I do think we're secretly sisters.) I also don't want to be the mom in that children's book who still goes over to her son's house when he's an adult and peeks into his window at night to check on him. (That's just creepy.)

I'm actually really excited about the day when my boys will have families of their own and plenty of babies to bring over for me to cuddle. As hard as it'll be to separate from them in a few years, I'm excited for the days when they'll start college classes, move to new places, start their own careers, make friends they'll keep for a lifetime, and grow into the men they were created to be. I can't wait to watch them graduate from college, launch their own art display at a gallery, design their first skyscrapers, release their first inventions, open the doors on their first businesses, or whatever it is they'll do. I don't want to be a wet blanket on their big plans or the rain on their parade. I don't want them to hold back or come up short from going after their biggest dreams because they think I'll be sad that they're leaving or changing too much or going too far away.

I want them to soar.

And I want to make sure I'm still their biggest cheerleader, still in their lives, still someone they can count on loving them and calling to ask how it's all going.

I want to be the warm hug they can always depend on, the person most interested in their plans and most excited to see them going after their dreams. I want to be the spunky 70-year-old they call when they're in their late 40s and looking for a shot of adrenaline to encourage them to do something amazing. I want to be the holder of the cup of tea when they want to visit after something hasn't gone their way, too.

I want the long haul, and I bet you do, too.

Just like you, I don't have a magic formula for making our

kids stay in a healthy relationship with us for their whole lives, but in this little chapter, I'm sharing the best ways I know to build the kind of family togetherness that lasts. With everything from playing a game and reading books aloud to talking about sex, drugs, and rock-and-roll and what to do when life throws a curveball, these tips hold the stories of the way I bond with my kids. I hope you will find something in these pages to inspire you. We may not have that magic formula, but we do have today. And today, we're going after the long haul.

I want to be the warm hug they can always depend on, the person most interested in their plans and most excited to see them going after their dreams.

Push the Family Reset Button

Some people unexpectedly leave a lasting impression on our lives. One of those people for me was a supervisor who taught me about pressing life's reset button — a practice with value I'm only now truly realizing.

The first time I met her I knew she possessed a magic I needed in my life.

Just a few years later, I got my chance and found myself working for her — an adventure that started when I walked into her office and saw a giant red and black button on her desk with the letters R-E-S-E-T scrawled on top. She caught me staring at it, picked it up, and said, "This is important. While working with me, you'll quickly discover that I make mistakes and you'll make them too, but here's the thing — we get to press the reset button as many times as we need to. It won't be easy, and you won't be perfect. Neither will I. But we'll always have this reset button, and we can start over again whenever we need to. Okay?"

Most people would love to hear a new boss say these words, but I was mortified.

"Me, make mistakes and need to start over? I don't think so," I wanted to say. (I was quite the perfectionist back then — before I knew better.) But as it turns out, she was right. I did make mistakes. I was out of my league, working a job that was way too advanced for my experience and training at the time. But, true to her word, when she or I messed up, we got to reset and start over with each other every time. I learned so much about grace during that season, and now, all these years later, I still think about that reset button, and I still have to press it from time to time, especially in my family life.

In fact, I had to use it this week for a hard family reset after making some serious mistakes.

It started a few weeks ago when I realized how horribly I had over-committed myself and felt like I couldn't do a thing about it. Instead of asking for help, I started letting stress make me into a frazzled person — wife, mom, friend, everything. Then, last weekend, my little guy asked me for a one-on-one several days in a row before I realized he wasn't asking for a trip to the ice cream shop; he seriously needed to talk to me. But I was too busy to listen, too frazzled from the craziness of my schedule to see the need written all over his face. Thankfully, he was persistent, and just one hour at a donut shop with him woke me up to my family's need for a hard reset.

As it turns out, life can be pretty stressful for every family member — not just the parents dealing with the logistics, but the kids who love those parents, too.

During that one-on-one while staring into his big brown eyes, I breathed deeply for the first time in weeks, forgot about everything else, and leaned into his amazing talent for telling stories. Then, I did the same thing with his brother the next day and got to sneak away with the hubs a few days after that. I refused to let mom guilt (or any other type of guilt) take over, and we started moving forward together.

I admitted my mistakes, apologized, and pressed my family's hard reset button and started making changes.

I realized that I had to give myself some grace or things would get much worse for all of us very quickly. So, we took a few days off from work and school, played some games, went hiking, made a plan for some things I was procrastinating, and started making things right again. And I thought about that old boss and how she taught me that grace is a requirement and perfection is a myth that can only hold power over us if we let it.

I'm not finished changing yet, but I'm so thankful for a family and friends who give me permission to press our reset button often, because striving for perfection doesn't work out nearly as well as grace — and it doesn't build nearly as much togetherness either.

If you need that permission in your own family, consider it granted today. If you need to,

- take a mental health day away from the norm
- go for a hike with someone you love
- read a good novel just because you want to
- get yourself to a really nice coffee shop
- eat the best pizza you can find
- treat yourself to a fancy haircut

- play a few family board games
- watch a movie marathon together

I hope you find your own family togetherness dreams coming into view.

Take a moment.

Think about what you do to reset things for your family when things go sideways. Make a plan now to make it easier when it happens.

When Life Throws a Curveball

The longer I'm on this planet, the more I realize that life rarely goes the way I plan. Whether it be in the form of a big announcement, a diagnosis, a dream deferred, a family member's outburst, or another something coming out of left field, it's safe to say that we've all been thrown for a loop by at least one or two curveballs in our lives.

In those moments when the you-know-what hits the fan, I often find myself wondering, **"How are we going to hold it all together?"**

And time after time, this is the number one thing that gets us through:

Lean in.
Listen.
Follow your gut.

It's so tempting to react, pull away, and panic (and I've definitely done my fair share of those), but when we lean in and listen instead, good things happen.

It's so tempting to spiral into a frenzy of indecision, call everyone I know for their advice, and sit in a sad, sorry pile of pity unable to move, but when I follow my gut and take a step forward instead, really good things happen.

Just like a mama bird follows her inner voice telling her when it's time to nest, hunt, and feed, what type of tree to choose, and where to lay her eggs, we have a guide in our guts if we listen to it.

Here's what it looks like in my corner of the world:

1 — As newlyweds in our early 20s, we found ourselves in a sticky financial situation when our first baby was on the way. We had to move out of a hopeless fixer-upper, and I knew I needed to quit my job and stay home with our baby, but there didn't seem to be a way. We asked our mentor at the time for advice, and he gave advice we knew wasn't right for us. So, I leaned into my husband, and listened to my heart. We crunched numbers, got moved, and I quit my job to stay home with the baby anyway — searching day and night for stay-at-home-mom jobs. It wasn't easy, but I knew I had to follow my gut no matter the cost, and it turned out to be one of the best decisions I've ever made. I know it's not the decision most moms make, but I couldn't shake the feeling that I needed to do it, so I did, and it changed my life in ways I still can't believe.

2 — A few years later, I was mama to two babies with all kinds of crazy good stuff happening in my life. But as I started looking ahead to the next 5 years with my hubby, we realized that the life we had built for ourselves would never help us reach our biggest hopes and dreams. We weren't thriving, and we knew it. We could have blamed each other, blamed the kids, or given up on our dreams, but instead, we took a deep breath, leaned into a few hundred hard conversations with each other, tried our best to listen,

and came away knowing what we needed to do to get back on track. It was weird and completely unconventional, and it was a hard decision to make. We knew our family and friends wouldn't completely understand, so we didn't tell anyone until the final papers were signed because we didn't want to be talked out of it. And even though we didn't know a soul living life the way we were about to live, we followed our gut and entered the world of full-time family travel. All these years later, we're so thankful we did.

3 — Now, as a mom of a teen and tween, when one of my kiddos tells me something is going wrong and it catches me off guard, I try my best to breathe deeply, wrap him up in a giant hug, and say "Tell me more" with everything within me. Then I listen hard and say the words, "We'll figure this out," and I write notes to remind myself to keep talking and listening in the days to come. We make lists, look for solutions, and do the research. I try to teach him about compromise, overcoming the tough stuff, and using his creativity to solve things. I let him teach me too. And then, I pray and write some more, dig deep, and make a decision. Do we need to make a change or give it more time? We make a decision. Do we need help or should we keep researching and trying solutions? We make a decision. I know I won't get it right every time, but I'm going to keep trying, because the alternative (sitting in a heap feeling sorry for myself) never works anyway.

Here's how I've seen these gems pop up for people I admire:

I've had the great privilege to do life with people who have leaned into me, listened to me, and taught me how to follow my gut — parents who told me I was smart enough to do anything and taught me how to trust God and follow His leading; a sister who believes I'm the expert even when I'm not; a husband who can tell when my mind is made up and who loves and supports me more than I ever knew I could be loved and supported; and friends, coworkers, and teachers who share their good times and bad times with me, showing me the value of engaging with people when I really want to run and hide, and modeling lives lived with God's Spirit as their guide. Doing life with these people has been the greatest teacher about leaning in, listening, and following my gut I could ever have.

And here's the CliffsNotes version for anyone skimming over those long paragraphs:

When something crashes the plan, close your mouth, open your heart, lean into your family, and search for that thing deep in your heart — the one thing you know you really want to do for your family. It just won't leave you alone, even though you're not 100% sure it's going to work out. Do it.
Find a way.
Make a way.
Be the way.
Follow your instinct. You'll be so glad you did.

And I'm right here with you.

Take a moment.

Write about your own go-to solution for when life throws you a curveball. What's your gut reaction? Are you happy with it or does it need a shift? How do you know?

Talk about Sex, Drugs, and Rock & Roll

Some topics make us uncomfortable — really uncomfortable. But so often those are the very topics we need to be talking about most with our kids. Why?

Because those are the areas where our kids need us the most.

They need a safe, trustworthy place to talk about sex, drugs, alcohol, and everything that goes with them. And we are that safe place.

No one likes talking about it. We might try to avoid the topic with our kids and try to talk as little as possible when the time comes, but research tells us that the price of not talking about these things early and often with our kids is high, and if we open up the conversation waves way before we're ready and way more often than we've ever considered — those uncomfortable conversations can be major connection points for our families.

Here's how.

It should happen in a lot of little conversations — not one big one.

In my house, we started talking about making wise choices around sex, saying no to pornography, drugs, and alcohol, and other sticky topics when my kids were about 6 or 7 years old, and we've been talking about them over and over ever since then.

Yes, I said 6 years old.

My kids are homeschooled, so I wasn't afraid they were going to hear something at school. They've always had pretty strict screen boundaries, so I wasn't extremely concerned about the screen risks at that age either. What made me start the conversation early and hold the communication lines open often was a big dose of wise counsel from other mamas and the research.

So, I thought I might share it with you today — just in case, like me, you tend to avoid the uncomfortable stuff.

The truth is that there are appropriate conversation starters for kids of all ages — from learning the names of body parts at age 1-2 to learning the difference between boys and girls at 3-4 and all the way to talking about how to search the internet safely, how to treat peers with respect, and what it means when someone in a movie says they "slept with" someone else.

We can try to avoid it, but there's a much better way — a way that builds togetherness — and it's as simple as this:

1. Normalize topics by inserting facts into all sorts of situations — book discussions, movie nights, while watching the news, one-on-one time together, family dinners, etc. (Need to know which facts to use? More on that below.)

2. Throw out the idea that it's one "The Talk" and embrace the fact that it's a bunch of talks over many years. It won't be one 60-minute monologue that helps kids make wise choices around drugs, alcohol, sex, pornography, etc. — it will be a collection of the little 5-minute ones. (This helps take the pressure off, too.)

3. Admit that the topic is uncomfortable and let them know it's okay to feel uncomfortable. Tell them it's your job as a parent to help them talk about things as they grow — it came with their instruction manual.

4. Let everything you say be the truth but realize you don't have to tell every single thing — you get to decide what's appropriate for the time.

5. MOST IMPORTANTLY, let them know you're a safe place to talk about it, to ask questions, and to build personal values together. Tell them you expect them to make wise choices and you're there to help them do that but let them know they can come to you when they make mistakes, too.

It really is that easy. Does it mean we have a 100% guarantee that our kids will always make the best choices? No — that's their responsibility. But it does mean that we can set them up for success and feel confident knowing we've done all we can.

Before we begin, we don't have to be experts, but we

should be as ready as we can be. That means we have some homework to do. To help, I'll share the tools we use in our house.

Here's the book series that helped our family:

- The **Learning About Sex series** from Concordia Publishing House with books on *Why Boys and Girls are Different* (ages 3-5) to *Where do Babies Come From?* (ages 6-8) and *How You Are Changing* (ages 9-12) to *Sex and the New You* (ages 12-14) and *Love, Sex, and God* (ages 14+) specifically for boys or girls

Here are recent resources I respect most on the topic:

- 5 Questions for Having the Talk With Your Kids — an article from iMom
- 3 Reasons You Should Want Your Child to Wait to Have Sex — an article from iMom
- The Birds and Bees Talk Moms Need to Have With Their Sons — an article from iMom
- What Your Kids Need to Know About Your Sexual History — an article from iMom (hint: it's not the details — it's something else)
- Honest Talk: How to Protect Your Kids from Pornography — a podcast Alicia Hutcheson did with Greka Eskridge
- 3 Reasons Why Parents Don't Want to Talk to Their Kids About Pornography and 3 Reasons They Should — an article by Greta Eskridge with so much wisdom and more great resources to help

- The Connection Between Sex Trafficking and Pornography
- The 7 Habits of Highly Effective Teens by Sean Covey — an old book I love reading during "Character Development" class with my kiddos

Here's the language we use in our home:

- "When on Google and YouTube, be so careful about choosing what to search and click. Watch out for bun-buns and let me know if you get onto something accidentally. Just close the computer and tell me that I need to close a page for you."
- "Your body is changing — that's God's way of growing you into a man/woman and preparing you to be a dad/mom one day. It's normal. It's natural. But it might feel strange to you. That's okay."
- "All choices have consequences — good ones and bad ones. You will have an opportunity to try drugs, alcohol, and sex outside of marriage one day. Let's talk about what those choices might lead to if you say yes or if you say no. Let's just roll it forward a few minutes, hours, years so you can make the best decision."
- "You can live a really happy life — these things don't have to be scary for you. That's why I want to tell you what the Bible says is the best way so you can make the best choices."
- "You are so smart. I know you can choose well, but if you make a mistake, don't be afraid to get help. We're always here to help."

Where does rock & roll fit into this equation? It doesn't really — that's just the way the saying goes, right — Sex, drugs, and rock & roll? But feel free to use it in your mini-talks if it feels right to you! (I'm not quite ready to expose my kids to some of the rap music I listened to back in 1999, but I'm sure they've probably already searched those songs on YouTube anyway.)

I know this tip wasn't the most fun to talk about, but talking about the sensitive, uncomfortable stuff with our kids is a great way to build a deep, lasting connection with them, and if sharing these resources with you can save even one family from the heartaches of unplanned pregnancy, alcoholism, human trafficking, substance abuse, abortion, or a similar tragedy, then the discomfort is totally worth it.

Take a moment.

Write out a few conversation starters you can use with your kids around these topics. Look for opportunities to start a five-minute conversation. Then another and another over the span of a few months or years. Envision yourself building that safe place for your kids to talk about these things. How does your face look when you're showing them it's safe to talk? How does it feel for them to be in the conversation with you?

Play a Game

"Forget about the rest — we're #gameschooling today." I say it about once a week, and in the past, I've felt at least a little guilty about it more often than not. The hashtag helps me feel less guilty, so I write it in my school planner — I'm sure my kids will laugh about that one day. But you know what? I've decided not to feel the least bit guilty about playing games with my family anymore.

Why? Because games count as learning in so many ways, and they're also magic for building family togetherness.

Whether we're playing something challenging like Scythe, Tokaido, Yahtzee, Catan, Dominion, Monopoly, Bananagrams, Chess, or Trekking the National Parks, or whether it's something silly like Exploding Kittens, Goat Lords, Spot It, or Bears vs. Babies, my family learns so much and grows closer together every single time we haul out the game boards.

Here's how.

How I know games count as learning:

- Almost all games teach math skills.
- Most games teach some form of strategy and critical thinking.
- You can use games to teach just about anything if you know where to look. (For details on this, I always consult one of the Homeschool Sisters —

Cait Curley. She's my favorite game-schooling guru.)

- Games let kids and adults play, which is critical to learning that lasts. (For more on that, check out B*ounce*, a documentary on the value of play)

How I know games build family togetherness in big ways:

- Smiles and heart-swells happen when the games come out in our home.
- Time with friends and extended family gets sweeter when there's a game involved. (Cornhole or putt-putt, anyone?)
- Eye contact increases exponentially during board games.
- We talk and laugh together so much when we're playing.
- Games work wonders with teenagers, too. (Games actually get more fun as kids get older, and they give us something fun to talk about together.)

Take a moment.

Come up with a list of games you love to play with your family. How long has it been since you played together? If it's been too long, make some time today.

Make Something Together

Every year when December rolls around, I feel like Charlie Brown — bombarded by the commercialism, trying to resist getting caught up in it, searching for the heart of the season, and angrily deleting every single sales email that pops into my inbox (and then digging them out of the Trash when I inevitably go shopping and need them).

And every single year, I end up having to remind myself to slow down, savor the good stuff, and let the rest go.

In those times when I get the most stressed about Christmas shopping, depleting bank accounts, and the gobs of stuff we're pressed to buy, some of the good stuff I try to hold onto is making things with my family. While we try to do it year-round, we also try to take extra time to make things together during the holiday season.

It's a great way to slow things down, make some memories, and give a few handmade gifts, too.

You know those super cool folks who can make even a toddler craft project look like an Instagram photo waiting to happen? I am **NOT** one of those people. In fact, if those folks were in the dictionary under "supercrafter" or "cool craft lady," you might just find my name listed as an antonym. I'm the kind of mama with glue in her hair and paint up to her elbows making even a well-planned adult art project look like a mess. It's always been one of my talents. But I don't let that stop me — I've been making a mess of art projects for decades now. Thankfully, some things turn out pretty well anyway, and when I'm making things with my family, the experience of making something together always turns into a huge togetherness win.

Whether we're baking cookies, painting a landscape, beading a necklace, or planting an herb garden, making things with our families is big for bonding.

If you're up for trying it and need ideas, here are a few we love:

- Paint pottery at a studio
- Bake cookies, cakes, quiches, whatever
- Draw maps, animals, video game characters, scenes
- Cook a meal and give everyone a dish to prepare
- Paint on canvas (it can be abstract if you're "challenged" like me)
- Redecorate a room, a house, anything
- Plant a seasonal garden
- Make figures out of Sculpey clay
- Build Lego minifigure shadowboxes
- Take a glass blowing class
- Put together a puzzle
- Buy an art project kit and complete it together
- Go to a painting, drawing, or pottery class
- Make glass fusion ornaments at a studio
- Write a song, a poem, a story, or a book
- Plan a trip, a surprise, a book club discussion, a party
- Design a website, a book cover, a business, a new type of clothing

- Sew or knit a scarf, a quilt, a sweater (I haven't braved this one yet, but I'll get there one day)

See what you can come up with — the possibilities are endless.

It's the experience you'll remember — the topics of conversation that come up, the moments of connection, the memories made that will last a lifetime.

In our house, we have one person who likes to make music (especially when he thinks no one else can hear him), one who loves to draw maps and trace detailed illustrations, one who loves to make his own toys out of Sculpey clay and play with them until they fall apart, and me with my paper bead necklaces. It's a hobby I've been dabbling in for years now, and I'm still trying to figure out exactly how to share it.

Take a moment.

Think about what you like to make with your family. Is it cooking a fancy dinner or dessert? Building treehouses or creating computer projects? What do your kids and husband love to make? Can they teach you how to help them? Take some time to make something together this week and see what happens.

Ask for Help

Sometimes a sink full of dirty dishes at the end of a very long day makes me want to cry, and when that happens, I hear these words echoing in my mind: "For the love of God, woman, just ask for help." I need to ask for help. My husband and friends tell me this all the time, but so often I just don't know how, and I know it hinders our family's togetherness factor.

It's been a major hang-up for me for a while now, and a quick Google search tells me I'm in good company — really good company. By just typing the words "moms asking for help," I found an article, tip, or trick from almost every major media outlet.

Lots of moms don't know how to ask for help, but unless we want to burn out and become total mom-zillas, we better figure it out.

Like most people who have a major hang-up, I blame this on something that happened when I was a kid. I don't know what happened exactly, but somewhere along the way while growing up I started resenting the ten million times every day I was called on to get something for someone. "Hand me my purse" or "Bring me my pen" became dirty words to me, and I started thinking that everyone should just take care of themselves and stop bossing other people around — especially kids.

So, I started out like a lot of women, doing all the mama things and taking on a whole host of housework and chores to boot. I had help along the way for sure, but I was always so guarded, insisting I should be able to do it all on my own. Now that I'm older, though, I'm discovering there are so many times I actually do need help, and because of that pesky hang-up, I really don't know how to ask for it.

I try to do everything on my own, and my heart grows bitter, resentful, and full of delusions of martyrdom — a recipe for the opposite of family togetherness if I ever saw one.

The weird thing is that my husband actually loves to cook and is great at it, and my kids are older now and pretty phenomenal at helping with cleaning, cooking, laundry, and all sorts of other things, and they need to learn how to do those things before they launch into college anyway. So why do I still feel like I should be the one doing it all?

This is something that has been bothering me for quite a while. On the really good nights, I pop on my noise-canceling headphones and listen to an audiobook while I tackle the overflowing sink of dirty dishes and tidy up the house for the next day, and then I cheerfully ask the boys to put away the dishes while I take a long, hot shower. I'm thankful to have a family to cook for and to have kids still living at home making messes to clean up, and I let my face show them how thankful I am for them.

But on the really bad nights, I stand at the sink staring listlessly out the window wondering why everyone else gets to have fun watching Netflix or playing video games for hours while I'm stuck in the kitchen making dinner and cleaning up after it. Then I get myself so worked up that I do all the chores myself, refusing everyone who offers to help but huffing and puffing enough to make everyone else miserable before I take a quick shower and collapse into bed. (You think I'm exaggerating, but my husband can tell you I'm not.)

So how can we find a way to ask for help so that our family togetherness can get back to being top-notch?

As usual, there's help on the internet. I took that Google search page and plucked out the best ones in case you might need help asking for help, too.

Here's what I found:

- Asking for help is letting someone else use their gifts, too.
- You need to ask for help — we all do. Get over it already.
- It's actually not faster and easier if you do it yourself.
- "Help" does not mean "I give up."
- Asking for help doesn't make us bad moms.
- Asking for help can be a sign of generosity and courage — not weakness.

I'm going to dig into these words of wisdom in the coming weeks. I'm determined to make a change.

Will you join me?

Because our families are definitely worth overcoming this fear of asking for help, aren't they?

Take a moment.

How have you learned to ask for help in a way that's not snippy, mean, or demanding? What stops you from asking for help most often? Write some notes to yourself about how you can handle this better in the future.

Read-Alouds and Bedtime Stories

Did you know it's impossible to grow out of bedtime stories and read-alouds? Reading aloud to younger kids brings them a sense of security, reading aloud with older kids brings deeper parent-child relationships, and reading aloud with your spouse can be really fun, too.

This was a revelation for me a few summers ago. I'd been taking my boys to the library since they were born, and we would always come home with stacks of books. Reading picture books aloud together when they were little was a powerful bonding tool for us. But when they got old enough to read confidently on their own, I stopped reading anything aloud to them that wasn't connected to school, and last summer I started to feel the disconnect.

That all changed when I read *The Read-Aloud Family* by Sarah Mackenzie and joined the tribe of parents at the Read-Aloud Revival reading aloud with kids of all ages.

If you want a simple way to get started in your home, ask the kids in your life which book they want to read aloud together and start reading aloud just a few minutes every night before bed. Or, select a book you know everyone loves and start reading it aloud together anytime. Pretty soon they'll be asking for just one more chapter or just one more book at all kinds of times during the day.

If that's not really your style, sign up for Audible and pop on an audio book for a while once a day, a few times a week, or whenever you're in the car together. We're Platinum members, which gives us two audiobooks every month for the price of membership and deep discounts when we want more than that, which we often do.

Or, if your kids are resistant at first (like my 12-year-old last summer), listen to books and podcasts by yourself or with your spouse, and let them know how much fun they're missing. After listening, you can share stories and book recommendations or strike up a conversation about a book you've both read and watch the connection happen. Or, as Sarah Mackenzie mentions in her book, you can pop on an audiobook for yourself in the car and see which kid gets interested in the story with you.

Start small and set something in motion. Then step back and watch it grow.

The folks over at the Read-Aloud Revival have loads of outstanding free book lists and ideas for all ages. One of the best things I've learned over there is about how to build a book club culture at home. It's changed the way we do breakfast in our house (now there always seems to be an audiobook around), and it's been a revolution to our homeschool in more ways than I can tell you.

You might be asking, "But how can we do this when we're already so busy?"

I had the same fears at first, but actually, read-alouds help us manage the overwhelm.

Here's an example: When we have a really busy day planned, we put on our audiobook while we're eating breakfast or while we're riding in the car, and just like magic, we're all whisked away to another world in two seconds flat and we have something new we're bonding over. Even if we only have 5-10 minutes, that's all it takes for everyone to build a connection that day.

My boys are barreling through middle and high school right now, and while connecting with them can be challenging sometimes, we're having so much fun together with read-alouds (especially on Audible). Between schoolbooks and the ones we're reading for fun, we always seem to have quite a few read-aloud books going at one time, which means loads of conversations, inside jokes, and family togetherness.

I can't begin to tell you how much connection has been restored to our family through reading aloud just since a few summers ago! I hope it does the same for your tribe.

Take a moment.

Make a list of books you'd love to share with your family. Hop online and find some book lists. (I suggest starting at readaloudrevival.com.) Ask your kids about their favorite books. Try an audiobook and see what happens.

Go on a Solo Adventure

I hate being alone for long periods of time. Actually, I really just hate being alone at all. I have no idea why.

Maybe it means I'm an extrovert since I'd rather recharge my personal batteries on a coffee date with someone I love than by being alone, or maybe it means I have personal issues I need to deal with and can't stand being alone with myself long enough to see them. Honestly, it's probably a bit of both.

Whatever the reason, I've hated being alone for as long as I can remember. In fact, during my first year of college, I was given the assignment to tackle my most difficult personal challenge, and I chose to eat alone in a restaurant. It was horrible for me. I also remember living alone in an apartment with no roommates for a few months and suffering from severe insomnia because of my loneliness and discomfort. This is odd, and I know it, and sometimes it's too much for my family.

In fact, I only just started understanding why this is too much for some of the people I love when I read Jamie Martin's amazing book *The Introverted Mom* earlier this summer. (Such a good book by the way, both for introverts and the extroverts who love them, too.)

But when I realized that my master's thesis was not going to write itself, and it wasn't going to be something I could do without a break from my normal weekend routine filled with all the good distractions of mom-life I normally love so much, I became crabby, snapping at the smallest of things, and I knew it was because I felt behind.

I hated to admit it, but I couldn't do it all. I was struggling, and everyone could see it.

So when my husband asked me how he could help, in a moment of desperation, I said, "The best-case scenario would be for me to shut myself in a beach cottage for a few days and get this over with." Moments later, he was on Airbnb booking me a place for the upcoming weekend all by myself.

I wanted to chicken out, to say I really didn't need it, to backtrack and ask for a redo, but I wouldn't let myself.

I knew I needed it — for my project and for my soul.

So, for the first time in too many years to count, I went on a solo adventure.

While I wish I could tell you it was filled with all the best hikes and beautiful scenic views from the highest mountains and that I met the most interesting people who were going to change my life forever, that's not what happened. Instead, I stayed in a tiny beach cottage with an Airbnb host I had never met before, and I closed myself in a room for hours on end, coming out only for fresh air, food, and exercise.

I wrote until my eyes crossed.

I watched every sunrise and sunset in complete silence.

I made coffee for one every morning.

I walked into town and ate lunch at a restaurant all by myself each day.

I even ate steamed spinach for breakfast, pie for lunch, and Cheez-its and hot tea for supper — something I would never do in my regular life.

I pretended to be a loner, spent a few hours looking at books in charming bookshops, bought two books I really didn't need and devoured them.

I wrote in my journal for hours about all of the things God had been trying to speak to me about for so long, but I'd been too busy to listen.

And I cried because I missed my family and felt guilty for needing this time away.

I wanted to go home early, but I made myself stay.

I missed my husband and my kids in a way I never have before, and I knew it was good for me. I was learning something that would change me, and I couldn't cut it short.

There was no one else to hide behind, nothing to take the pressure off of myself, no way to pretend I was invisible or just a part of someone else's story. The story was just me all weekend long getting stuff done and searching for whatever God would say to me exactly the way a man with his head on fire searches for a bucket of water (as Elizabeth Gilbert would say).

And you know what? I survived. Actually, I did more than survive.

I got over the hump in my project and came away with something that made me a better wife, mom, friend, sister — a better me better equipped for time with my family.

I came away with a big dose of gratitude.

I wanted to clean a sink of dishes the people I love had dirtied. I wanted to pick up toys off the floor, the couch, the bed, anywhere. I wanted to be distracted by the sound of "Mama, come look at this!" or "Hey honey, have you read this yet?" I wanted the mess that is my life— every single bit of it. In fact, I longed for it so much that my soul ached.

At the end of the weekend, I breathed in deep my last moments of solitude. It was good to be going back home to my people, good to have such an intense longing for them, good to let this deep sense of gratitude and ache for them seep into my bones, and so good to know that I could sit there alone and be okay too. More than that, I could go home confident, strong, and comfortable in my own skin.

The truth is that during those days alone, I started to realize just how much I've grown since my college days when I hated being alone so much. These people I get to spend my life with every day have changed me.

They've made me a better version of myself.

I don't rely on them for my life's meaning or to have something to vicariously live through. I don't rely on them to take some of life's pressure off of myself. I rely on them because they rely on me, and I am stronger because of it.

I need them because they need me, and I'm better for it.

If you ever find yourself realizing you haven't felt that deep gratitude and longing for your family in a while, I'm sending you my biggest hopes that you will do whatever you can to find it again. I hope you can find a way to have a solo adventure of your own, or however you get your gratitude mojo back — whether that be a weekend away or a few hours alone in your own house, a solitary lunch at a coffee shop or a few nights away on a business trip — and that you'll come back with a new passion for your family too.

Take a moment.

What holds you back from taking a solo adventure to refresh yourself? Does it make you feel afraid to consider it? What do you think would happen if you were alone for a while? Write about it.

Let Your Face Light Up

Being a parent can be overwhelming sometimes. Totally and completely worth it, but still overwhelming. We want our kids to be the happiest, most well-mannered, well-behaved kids on the planet. We want them to be smart, kind, caring, compassionate, and to knock everyone's socks off with how beautiful and handsome they are, too.

We want them to be well-rounded, well-read, well-traveled, and to have the very best shot at the best colleges and careers on the planet.

In the meantime, we wash their dishes, cook their meals, do their laundry, clean their bathrooms, help with homework or homeschool, work jobs to put food on their tables, and read books, scour websites, and listen to podcasts about how to do it all a little bit better.

In the midst of it all, we might wonder, "Am I missing something important?"

At the end of the day, we want a true, lasting connection with our kids — whether they're 1, 11, 21, or 51. We want to hold them close, to let them fly, to have a family life where every single day is an adventure we all want to be on together.

We want a relationship with them above all else, and we want that relationship to be strong and lasting, long after they have children of their own and we're not doing their laundry anymore. Sometimes, even in the throes of parenting young ones, everything else fades as this one true goal comes into focus.

And we realize there's something that needs to change.

For me, this happened in 2007 when I watched a 64-second interview with Toni Morrison about how one small motherhood tweak changed everything for her. It's called "Does Your Face Light Up?" And during those 64 seconds as I heard Toni Morrison's story, over 12 years ago now, I made that same small tweak, and it's changed everything for me, too.

It might sound small and simple, but I promise you, it makes a profound difference.

Letting your face light up.

It's letting a smile take hold of your entire being in the morning when your kids stumble down the stairs or hop into your bed.

It's grinning from ear to ear when you get back from a walk alone and wrapping them up in a hug.

It's locking eyes with your husband when he walks through the door and giving him a big smile and smooch.

It's recovering from a moment of sheer overwhelm with a genuine look of love toward your little ones.

It's letting your face light up every single time you see the ones you love, focusing on their faces, their smiles, and their shining eyes instead of their untucked shirts, muddy shoes, or messy hair.

I certainly haven't mastered this, but I'm working on it. And even after all this time, I still think about that clip so much, realizing the power of something as small as the look on our faces, realizing that even a smile can change everything for our kids, especially on the toughest of days.

Take a moment.

Let the ones you love delight you. Let your smile show them how much. Set a reminder on your phone if you have to. Do whatever helps you remember. You'll be so glad you did.

Refuse to Multi-task

I deleted my email apps from my phone yesterday — all of them, even the ones for work. Maybe that wouldn't be a big deal for you, but for me, it was earth-shattering — something I didn't think I'd ever do.

But as I flipped through my email on my phone with one hand, filled the kettle for coffee with the other, and put an eye on the computer trying to check on a project, an ear towards a story my little boy was telling me, and a separate train of thought trying to make a to-do list for the day, an article called "Single Tasking is the New Black" in *Best Self Magazine* stopped me in my tracks, and I realized it was time to make a change.

In that one instant, I started to see that all of my efforts for family togetherness were being undermined by my determination to do multiple things at once. All. The. Time. Multitasking is a survival tactic I've been employing for several years now — the only thing I thought was allowing me to be super productive in so many areas of life. And honestly, it felt like it was working for such a long time. Until all of a sudden, it didn't.

The truth is, I've been feeling my family (and my brain) rebel against my multi-tasking for about a year now, and I've been ignoring it.

My kids are always waiting for me to finish just one more email, to complete just one more task, to wrap up just one more phone call. They've gotten used to me not being able to watch a movie all the way through with them because I need to just finish the dishes "real quick." They've seen me glance at my phone at 10 pm for just one more check right before bed and end up problem-solving in my head while trying to focus on snuggling or chatting with them.

Meanwhile, my heart and mind have been longing for a reprieve — longing to focus on one thing at a time. Migraines knock on my doorway too often. I alienate friends because my brain can't focus on their stories. My kids know when my brain is overloaded and I'm not listening to them because my eyes glaze over and I just smile and nod.

Over the past few months, so many quotes and articles have come my way telling me it's time to stop. NPR calls multi-tasking a human delusion and talks about it causing stress on the brain that can be dangerous. *Psychology Today* claims that it takes more time to do things when we multi-task than it would take to focus on singular tasks individually. *Forbes* magazine names multi-tasking as the enemy of productivity. Somehow, even with all of this evidence to the contrary, I thought my brain was different.

And then, yesterday's article made me see the impact on my family — the straw that broke the camel's back.

The article came from one of my favorite email groups — the Best Self tribe I became a part of a few years ago, and here's the quote that prompted me to action:

"I really did believe that multi-tasking was my superpower. I mean, there were so many benefits, I never thought this juggling would ever hinder me. Fast forward a decade and a half later and I will tell you that not one of the handful of tasks I ever did at once got the attention it deserved. *If I am being completely honest, my kids probably suffered the most. I can't imagine what went through their little heads…*"
— Melinda Andrison

As soon as I saw those words, I realized that even with all the things we do to build connection and family togetherness, my own kids and husband suffer when I try to do so many things all in the same moment. They feel less-than, not as important, pressured, bored, and hurt, and only I can make things different. So, I am.

Here's how:

- From now on, when I listen to a story, I'm going to close everything and really listen.
- When I watch a movie, I'm going to forget about everything else.
- During the hours when I'm working or writing or answering email, I've blocked out time to do it, and I'm not trying to do anything else.
- I won't assess my to-do list during meals.
- I won't write emails in my head during breakfast.
- When we're homeschooling, I'm fully engaged or doing something else close by, ready to put it down when a question comes my way.

- I won't try to do just one more thing "real quick" — I'll block off time and be intentional about my attention.
- When I'm on a phone call, the kids are engaged elsewhere.

And now that you know I'm trying, there's no turning back, right? If the experts are right, my brain fuzz will dissipate, my productivity will soar, and my family will win.

Take a moment.

How do you feel about multitasking? Could you ever survive without it? What would it feel like to take up the habit of single tasking?

Fill Your Home with Laughter

How often do our loved ones hear us laugh, chuckle, giggle, or give a big belly laugh? It's a question I never used to ask myself until one day, years ago, my mom caught me off-guard by saying, "It does my heart so good to hear you belly laugh. I haven't heard it in a while."

It was sobering as I started to realize that I'd been so focused on making sure everyone was clean, fed, dressed, happy, and safe that I'd forgotten that my life was supposed to include me having a good time too. I still felt joyful, thankful, and happy with my life, so what was the problem?

The problem was that I had lost my laugh. I promptly set about getting it back.

I bet you've been there too — traveling through one of life's seasons where laughter isn't your go-to response.

Or maybe you're there right now.

With a couple of hard weeks stacking up together, it would be understandable if laughter didn't happen a lot right now. People we love are out of work, news headlines display a dismal outlook, and social media is out of control. I'd be lying if I said I didn't wake up and want to hide under the covers a day or two this week.

But do you know the one thing I've heard from countless families bringing them back together and grounding them in family togetherness no matter the season?

Filling our homes with laughter.

It might not be easy for any of us right now. There's so much uncertainty, plenty to be stressed about, and so much to read, research, and wonder over, but the other day, something happened that made me realize just how important laughter is for family togetherness. It was a simple phrase from one of my kids:

"Mama, I really like hiding and finding stuff with you. It's so funny."

He was talking about the way we like to hide a gnome, an Olaf pop figure, or an old Beanie Baby in random places around the house for each other to find — a simple game he started a few months ago that has brought us all so much laughter. When I wake up in the morning, I might find a funny Olaf figurine where my glasses should be, or when I go to make coffee, I might find a gnome staring back at me. It really is funny, but until he said that, I didn't realize just how much it meant to him that I was playing along and laughing too.

Isn't it wonderful how the smallest things can make such a big impact?

What kind of things make your family laugh?

What's your style? What kind of thing lightens up your home? I bet if you think hard enough you can remember something that brought giggles in the past.

Here are a few ideas to try:

- Dance to a song or two
- Set a reminder to laugh every day
- When a spill happens, choose laughter over scolding
- Crack a joke or play a silly game
- Watch a funny movie or YouTube video
- When someone says something they don't mean, choose laughter over offense

Whatever you do, make sure you're laughing too. It's bound to bring deep connection when you do.

Togetherness is about so much more than being in the same room with someone. It's about connection, intentionality, and presence — and that's something we all can do.

Take a moment.

Think about what fills your home with laughter. Make a plan to do one funny little thing today and see who chuckles. Hopefully it'll be you.

5

Getting Back Up Again

"Start over, my darling. Be brave enough to find the life you want and courageous enough to chase it..."
— *Madalyn Beck*

The night of my 30th birthday, I crept into my boys' room to kiss them goodnight. As I watched them drift off to sleep, I heard a voice deep inside me say, "It's too late for you. Forget about your dreams and settle into making things better for your kids instead. They've got a shot, but you already missed yours." It had been a tough few years, and I was getting frustrated at the way life was turning out. I loved my husband and our little boys so deeply, but I felt like our life was nothing more than a series of false starts, failed dreams, obligations, and expectations. I didn't feel like we were really becoming who we were meant to become.

I wanted to get my master's degree, but we didn't have the

money. I wanted to live by the ocean, but we had just bought a house and secured jobs in the middle of the state. I wanted to see the world with my family, but there didn't seem to be a way. I wanted to be a writer, but I had a good job that paid the bills as a — wait, what was my job again? It seemed like a foreign reality compared to my family and the dreams in our hearts. We had lived overseas and come home, but we didn't fit in at home anymore. We had been leaders in the church on a path to great influence and significance, but we'd walked away from that — not really fitting in there either.

At first, I thought the voice was God telling me that I should be a responsible parent and stop thinking about my own dreams so that I could raise the little world changers under my roof. Parenthood does involve sacrifice, right? Thankfully, though, I scratched that idea pretty quickly, knowing that voice was something else. It was my fear, my laziness, my resistance, and I wasn't about to listen to it. It's tragic to think that walking away from our dreams is the best thing we can do for our children. On that lonely night in my babies' bedroom, I had a choice to make and the choice I made was to believe that the *opposite* is true — giving up our dreams isn't the best thing we can do for our kids; becoming fully alive is the best thing we can do for them — no matter how many times we fail, falter, stumble, or stagger forward.

Now, almost a decade later, I'm still reeling at how close I was to sinking into the failure mentality, how close I was to losing part of myself by falsely believing it was selfish to be a big dreamer. It's not too late for a 30-year-old to go after her dreams any more than it's too late for a 5-year-old to go after hers. And no matter how old we get or how many times we fall down, it will never be too late for us to go after our dreams.

In the years since that moment, I'm thankful to say that I've gotten my master's degree, moved with my family to the coast (actually to several different coasts), and I've become a writer, too. But that doesn't mean things have been easy. I could go on for pages to describe the challenges we've faced, but I won't. Most recently, those challenges looked like this: I failed my Master's thesis and had it downgraded to non-publishing status just so I could graduate (yep, me, the former Valedictorian and *summa cum laude* girl), and as I sit in my tiny home this morning writing these words, my family is just a few months into recovering from our biggest family dream ever gone wrong (and the resulting 6 months of being uncomfortable and displaced). But I'm still thankful that I decided to be a big family dreamer — and a big dreamer for myself, too.

Every time I hear one of my kids talking about how they'd like to live in Greece or spend some time in Italy one day, every time I hear them chatting away about the possibilities of space travel or the cool innovations and inventions that could revolutionize medicine or architecture or change history, I'm thankful I didn't stop dreaming big when they were little. Even when I hear them say, "How about we never try to live on a boat again; okay, Mama?" or "Hey, can we slow down traveling for a little while?" and the mom guilt starts to wash over me, I remind myself that making mistakes and falling flat on our faces only happens to those of us who try new things. So, I smile, help them deal with anything they're struggling with, and we talk about what a great learning experience failure truly is, making a plan to do it better next time.

Have you ever gone after a big dream and fallen flat on your face, too? Have you ever felt like your dream wasn't important enough, wasn't achievable enough, wasn't timely enough to go after in the first place? Or are you so afraid of disappointment, failure, and regret that you've been holding yourself back from your destiny for far too long? Do you feel like you're too old, too tired, too busy, or too something else to go after that one thing you've had in your heart since you were a kid? Too stuck in a rut to have the family life you really want?

If that's you, you're going to love this last chapter of the book. Here I'm sharing togetherness tips all about embracing disappointment and starting again, keeping your heart grateful when things go wonky, knowing when it's time to go home again, and learning how to step up and move forward even when it's hard.

I used to hate it when people would tell me that everyone has either been through a hard time or they're about to go through one. It filled me with dread, worry, and enough anxiety to fill a swimming pool. So I won't tell you that. Instead, I'll tell you that I hope you don't go through hard times. I hope you learn from the mistakes of others and make so many great choices that you get to avoid many of life's hardships. And I'll also tell you that if you should find yourself encountering disappointment one day, there is a way forward.

There's always a way forward.

I hope you find some inspiration for that way forward in these pages.

becoming fully
alive is the best
thing we can do
for our
children,
no matter how
many times we
fail, falter,
stumble, or
stagger forward

Embrace Disappointment and Begin Again

When I started sharing these Togetherness Tips with you, I never thought I would be writing to you about embracing disappointment. I honestly did not see disappointment as a part of chasing big family dreams or building a deep connection with our families — probably because I've been trying to avoid it my whole life.

Then, a few weeks ago, these words captured me:

> *"Some people resent being challenged by life. They think challenges should not exist. But if you have lived long enough, at some point you realize that the world isn't here to make you happy. It can't do that . . . We need the crisis. There are two levels of truth. One is to see the craziness of what's happening now. And another is to see, from a higher perspective, that what's happening now is part of our evolution."* — Eckhart Tolle in Oprah's *The Path Made Clear*

Ouch. I quickly recognized myself in that first line and knew I needed a shift in perspective. What I didn't realize was how quickly I was about to get it.

It's not that I've never been disappointed before; I certainly have. I've experienced my share of deep disappointment and loss over the years, but somehow, I still thought my life and my family would be altogether better if I tried to avoid it as much as possible. I chase family togetherness and big family adventure like a crazy person — going from this big dream to that one, so there's not much time left to sit with my disappointments.

Then, in the winter of 2019, our big family adventure was derailed, my husband was facing a serious health issue, my master's thesis was rejected, and I found myself dealing with major disappointment.

I thought I could make it better by working harder. So, I pushed myself to another new limit on all fronts and thought that would fix everything — but it didn't. This time, disappointment couldn't be avoided — my husband needed time to heal, we couldn't travel like we wanted to, my thesis was rejected again, my graduation postponed another semester, and my confidence was dipping to an all-time low.

But I'm a high achiever, and failure is not in my DNA, so I thought I could at least get my thesis approved by pushing extra hard for just 5 more days to make it happen the way I had planned.

The result was a lingering migraine that left me on my back with nothing left to do but pray, and I knew I had 2 choices: I could either keep pushing for the dream to happen just exactly the way I thought it would and become a hot, sick, tired, crabby mess, OR I could embrace the disappointment as a vital part of my growing and maturing process and begin again in a healthy way.

I didn't want to begin again. I didn't want to embrace disappointment either. And I certainly didn't want anything to mess up the plans I had made. But more than that, I desperately did not want to be a hot, sick, tired, crabby mess for my family.

So, I closed my laptop and decided to do the only thing that really helps me when things go sideways — lean into my family. We carved out time for a movie night, did some shopping, ate some froyo, went for a long walk (and rescued a sick lizard as a result), worked on a puzzle, and read a few fun books aloud.

And then I started to see it — I started to see disappointment as a gift for big family dreams and big family togetherness, too.

I thought about all of us who have dealt with big blows of rejection — the dream job that never happened, the book publisher rejection letter, the friendship that never blossomed, the negative diagnosis for a child, the difficult decision to drop out of an election, race, or program that's been a dream since childhood. I thought about the humility we gain when these things happen, the perspectives that shift, the immense room these things make for the things that really matter.

And a thought dropped into my mind: What if, when we embrace disappointment, we're choosing a better path altogether? What if this was the way it was really supposed to be from the start?

What if this disappointment is actually a God-appointment for something better?

What if that dream job would only truly be a dream next year when you come back and apply again with more experience and maturity? Or what if it wouldn't have been a dream job at all and you need to knock on a different door? What if the book publisher rejection letter leads you to find a different publisher — the one that's a better fit for you? What if the friendship that isn't blossoming right now might blossom next month or next year or with someone else who would be a better friend for you later? What if that negative diagnosis leads you to lean into your child in a way you never would have otherwise, and you find out that the bond you've built is something that will last a lifetime? What if leaving the election, race, or program this year means that next year you'll come back and knock it out of the park with a new idea you never could have had without that first drop-out?

What if we become more human — more full of grace, more truly ourselves — when we deal with disappointment and begin again than we ever could be if everything went right all the time?

And what if that makes us more equipped for family togetherness and big family dreams?

It's a scary thought at first — the idea of beginning again, the thought that there could be something much different and much better than our little minds can envision right now. At the end of the day though, we absolutely will not stop chasing the big dreams in our hearts. We might just be a little more open to the idea that those big dreams might need to come about another way — a better way.

Take a moment.

Consider how you deal with disappointment and find a way forward. What is one thing you've learned from past disappointments? Have you found your way to being thankful for them yet?

Keep Your Heart Thankful

As I write this, it's the morning after Thanksgiving and the pumpkin pie is nearly gone at my house, but my heart still isn't as thankful as it should be.

I know I should be thankful.

I know I have so much to be thankful for.

I know that thankfulness is so important when it comes to building connection with our families. I also know that it's not the happy people in this world who are thankful but the thankful people who are happy, along with so many other wise words I've used for years to help people who aren't seeing their many blessings.

But two big blows have come my way recently, leaving me shaken to my core. So today, I'm having to fight to feel thankful, and I'm just not quite there yet.

Maybe you can relate?

I will get that thankful heart — don't you worry — but first, a little bit about what happened.

The first blow was to me personally — an email waiting in my inbox from my graduate school advisor informing me that the thesis project I had invested a year into had a major flaw that escaped notice until two weeks before the due date, leaving me with mounds of work to redo and the realization that my dreams of publication were toast. I won't go into details on the pity party I had for myself that day, but trust me, it was ugly, and it ended with me under a fuzzy blanket in the middle of the day creating a pool of tears on my bed. Thankfully, the pity party only lasted about 10 minutes, but the impact on my heart is still there today.

Then, just a few days later, the *big* blow came. "I just feel weird" is definitely not what anyone wants to hear from her husband, especially if that weird feeling has been increasing for more than a few weeks. A few doctor's visits and a quickly scheduled surgery later, and then we were hearing words we never thought we'd hear: "There's only about a 1% chance this isn't cancer." I was the one who fell apart — not him — and then I was the one dealing with guilt for not being strong enough, for not dealing with this well enough, for being so selfish. Thankfully that nasty C-word is now removed from his body and the doctors say we have no reason to think it's present anywhere else because of how soon he got to a doctor, but he's still recovering physically and we're all still recovering emotionally. And even though I know I'm especially struggling because I just lost my mom to that same nasty C-word just 13 months ago, it still shakes me that I'm not as strong as I thought I was.

The truth is, though, that no matter how hard it is, we have to fight for thankfulness long after the pumpkin pie is gone, every single year.

Because thankfulness makes us better spouses, better parents, better friends.

Thankfulness makes us better changemakers, better contributors to this world, better versions of ourselves.

Thankfulness is also an act of worship, a spiritual practice, and one of the very best ways we can give back to the One who created us and gave us so much to be thankful for in so many ways.

So, if you ever want a little extra help building thankfulness into your life long after that pumpkin pie is gone in your house,

Here are a few things you can try:

1 — Waking up early to exercise, read, pray, and listen to a song that means something to you

2 — Setting aside time to talk to someone you're thankful to have in your life

3 — Participating in a gratitude writing exercise or two

4 — Finishing a good book

5 — Hopping onto your favorite blogs and perusing Pinterest to find scripture, inspirational quotes, more gratitude prompts, and other advice for getting your gratitude mojo back

Already as I write this, I'm realizing how much I really do have to be thankful for, and that is such a blessing. Just the fact that I have the opportunity to write to you, a warm home to write from, to be able to even go to graduate school (and eventually finish), and to have a family and friends who love me is enough to knock me into thankfulness gear at least a little bit.

Take a moment.

Take some time to think about how you keep your heart thankful when things don't go your way and how much it matters to your family.

Journal Your Heart Out

We've probably all heard the saying, "If you don't have anything nice to say, don't say anything at all." I've used it with my kids at least a hundred times. But let's face it — sometimes if we want genuine togetherness in our family relationships, we need to say things we know may not go over well, and there may not be a very nice way to do it. On top of that, sometimes we feel grumpy or have hormones that aren't helping us either. In those moments, I think we have three choices:

We can fly off the handle, bottle it up and wait for a better time, or find a way to say it with the love they deserve.

I don't think anyone would recommend flying off the handle, but I may have just a bit of experience in the "bottling it up" category and I can tell you that while waiting for a better time can certainly be a good idea, "bottling it up" long-term is extremely unhealthy. (Don't ask me how I know.) So, that just leaves finding a way to say it with the love they deserve.

The good news is that while we may only have one shot with the words that leave our lips, we have an unlimited amount of practice available in our journals.

If you're a part of our email group, remember the e-book you received when you joined "10 Surefire Ways to Build

Togetherness into Your Everyday"? Number 9 on that list is SAY HARD THINGS, and it certainly applies here:

"Being willing to say the hard things means immediately trading a heavy heart for a light one; it means not wasting even one second or forfeiting even one ounce of the joy that is possible. By saying the hard things today, we are giving ourselves the gift of time with the ones we love, because when we're willing to face things head-on and get the clutter out right away, we have so much more left to give."

Have you ever found that to be true? I wish I could get back all the time I've wasted in the past when I felt like I couldn't say what I needed to. There's truly so much freedom and so much more room for genuine connection when we're able to get that thing off our chest, but you probably already know that doesn't give us permission to say hard things fresh off the presses of our brains. Instead, we may need some time to get the words out right.

That's where journaling comes in. Here are a few journaling prompts to help us wade through our cluttered minds and let our hearts shine through:

- What would you say if you had to talk about this at this very second? Write it out with a pencil (slow and steady).
- What words would you use to talk about this if you knew you wouldn't be interrupted? Write them all down.

- Read through and cross out anything that's not entirely what you mean. Cross through the things most likely to be misinterpreted.
- Read through the words slowly and put yourself in the receiver's shoes.
- How would it make you feel to hear this from someone you love?
- Are there pieces you can reword?
- Which parts need to be said now and what needs to wait?
- How could you say what you need to say more clearly?
- Can you find the love shining through yet? If not, start over again.

I bet you could add to that list of prompts, but I hope this helps generate a few ideas the next time you need to say something difficult in your family.

I hope you're able to keep your heart light and say what you need to say to the people you love. And I hope you know that whether it's "I love you" or "I'm so thankful for you" or something a little more like "I'm not sure you're listening to me" or "Can we talk about something difficult?", you have someone cheering you on.

Take a moment.

Think about it: How do you prepare to say hard things to the people you love when you need to?

Take Care of Yourself

Last Friday, as soon as I hit the send button on our togetherness tip, I started thinking about what we haven't talked about yet together, and I was overcome with a realization. As I was thinking about what stands in my way of getting family togetherness right so many times, it hit me like a freight train:

It's so hard to show respect, speak with kindness, and prioritize togetherness with the people we love the most when we don't feel our best.

Here's my story…

August 18 probably doesn't seem like a super-important day to most people. It's not the traditional time to set a new course for one's life or to set resolutions, new diet plans, new exercise regimes, or anything of the sort. But last year, on August 18, after seeing a passport photo of myself that looks like I got stung by a bee and is seriously scary enough to make babies cry, I decided I had to start taking better care of myself in a big way, and it's made all the difference in the world.

I wish I could tell you that was the first time I'd had to make that decision in my life.

The truth is that I've made deep and drastic changes for my health several times as an adult, done really well for months and months, and then totally fallen off the wagon in a spiral of processed foods, sleep deprivation, and lack of exercise that left me right back in unhealthy mode.

Now, all these months later, I feel like a new person.

I've dropped all kinds of inches and inflammations, sworn off meat completely and am consistently choosing fruits and veggies over dairy and gluten, and I've prioritized exercise, prayer, and even taken up meditation.

But I can see that fork in the road again — if I allow history to repeat itself, it's time for me to go back to my old ways again.

But guess what? This time, I won't do it.

How do I know? Because this time I have help. And I'm sharing that help with you in case you could use a few boosters to help you take care of yourself too.

Here are 5 big buckets of resources to help us be our best for our families:

1 — Guard our hearts.
If we're going to take care of ourselves, we have to start with our hearts. For me, a lot of that is watching what I read. A few weeks ago, I was listening to an audiobook about achieving personal and professional goals, and the author talked about her family like this, *". . . and then the hellions down the hall wake up. . ."* I was disgusted and my mood was wrecked for more than a few hours. Eventually, I had to stop and ask myself why I was so fired up, angry,

and incensed by these words, and I discovered it was because this book has been read by thousands and thousands of women already and is receiving a lot of attention right now, and it's filled with phrases that encourage women to consider their children as distractions from their best work. I should've just stopped listening to the book right then, but I didn't. I let myself get even more fired up by finishing the thing, and I may have bought Girl Scout cookies that very same week and gotten a little off-track in my healthy food choices. Coincidence? I think not. If you're like me and you need to watch what you read to guard your heart, my biggest suggestion is to reach out to trusted sources for book recommendations that promote family-loving principles. I have quite a few friends online who give stellar book recommendations, and I call on them regularly.

2 — Guard our minds.

I know there are some of you out there that may not love personal development articles, books, podcasts, and social media accounts as much as I do, but no matter how you feel about them, I bet you can at least agree with me that we're all filling our minds with something. Whether it's conversations with friends, news, Netflix, or television sitcoms (or maybe even books would fit here for you — they're probably not in the heart category for everyone), what goes into our minds eventually comes out of our mouths and spills over our families over and over again. So, we have to take special care in guarding what goes into our minds to keep control of what comes out of our mouths.

I could go on and on in this category to tell you how

thankful I am that we quit cable television over six years ago or how worried I am that my kids' love for shoot-em-up video games will leave them talking about strange things I can't understand for years, but instead, I'll leave you with the one way I guard my own mind whenever I find my own mouth saying things I don't want to say — I go on a walk, pray, read Scripture, and plug into the most positive, truth-giving friend or personal development podcast or audiobook I can find. Then, before I know it, I'm out of my funk, finding myself speaking more like the fountain I want to be instead of the drain I sometimes am.

3 — Eat more green stuff (and less of everything else).
When we sort through all of the hoopla about diet plans and weight loss and which foods do this or that for our bodies, the food element of taking care of ourselves really seems to boil down to one thing — eat more of the good stuff and less of the rest. You may have your own gurus that you love, and I say get back to them (and share them with me!). The two books that I go back to again and again for help with this are Kris Carr's *Crazy Sexy Diet* and Joel Fuhrman's *Eat to Live*. If I'm tempted to go for the animal products because I'm feeling super hungry, I go to these two books for a plant protein recipe. If I'm feeling extra depleted, I look at these two books for vitamin recommendations. And for me, at the end of the day, there's very little that can't be solved with a good recipe and a big dose of water, sunshine, green smoothies, and a few Vitamin C and B gummies.

4 — Move our bodies.
It really is so important to get out and move our bodies for

at least 30 to 60 minutes every single day. There are literally hundreds of research studies showing how important it is to exercise daily and how much damage we do to ourselves by refusing to make it a priority. Back problems, hip problems, blood pressure problems, heart problems, and all sorts of other issues pop up when we don't prioritize moving our bodies, and then, those problems make us feel like not moving, so the cycle just goes on. We can literally reverse all of that by moving our bodies more every single day. Walk, run, dance, hike, join a gym, go to a class, park a mile away from where you're going and walk, or if you tend to be on the shy side, take up a yoga practice with an app like Down Dog. Start with 10 minutes a day, then 15, then 20, and before you know it, you'll be moving 60 minutes every single day. You don't have to do it all at once either — take the baby for a 10-minute walk around the block six times a day, go around the block a time or two between meetings or after every meal, take the stairs a few extra times, do whatever you have to do to get moving. I bet you'll feel the difference the very first day.

5 — Get our zzz's.

I'm not a big sleeper. Sources say I never have been. So, I normally run best on 5 to 6 hours of sleep every night for a while and then my body rebels and I have to do 9 to 10 hours for a few nights to catch up. I hate it, but it keeps me humble and helps me stay productive, so I guess it works. No matter what your sleep routine is, I bet you can feel it when you haven't had enough sleep in your life (and our families can feel it, too). When I'm not getting enough sleep, it colors my whole day dark. If you ever struggle with sleep, I hope you already have an arsenal of help, but just in case you don't, here are my go-to remedies:

- Water — so much water
- Pile on the exercise — 90 to 120 minutes a day
- Unplug the TV for at least a week
- Shut down social media for days, weeks, or months
- Dump your brain in a paper journal (get those ideas out)
- And if you struggle with insomnia, please see a professional with a good holistic mindset — I struggled with this in college and didn't get the help I needed. Reach out, Mama!

And that's it — those are the best ways I know to take care of ourselves so that we can be at the top of our game, feeling our best, and able to give all kinds of love to the people we love the most.

Take a moment.

Write down a few things that help you feel your best. What gets your heart pumping? What leaves you with enough endorphins to power good family togetherness for days?

Who Said You Can't Go Home Again?

Going after big family dreams don't work out is risky.

Whether you want to shift your life so you can spend more time with your family or go on a one-time epic family adventure, there are certain risks involved.

When we went after our dream of living on a catamaran this past fall, we were all-in. We put all of our eggs in the catamaran basket, left our Airstream home in winter storage in Maine, and plunged head-first into making it work. (We even came close to selling our truck because we were so sure we wouldn't need it.) When people asked us what we would do if we didn't like living on a boat or if something went sideways and we couldn't sail back up to Maine as we had planned, we laughed and said that wasn't possible. We'd been dreaming about and planning for this for over three years — how could it not work?

This wasn't the first time we had gone all-in on a family togetherness dream, so we thought we had a pretty good formula for making big, risky stuff work. We'd pushed through financial hardship to live in Australia when we were in our early 20s. We'd broken out of some pretty deep ruts to travel full-time in our Airstream when we were in our early 30s. So, we thought it was time to burst into our early 40s by learning to sail and living on a catamaran. But, as you may already know, things change, especially when health challenges arise. Priorities shift. Stress becomes the enemy, and health takes a front seat.

As it turns out, this wasn't the right time to go after our big catamaran dreams, so we had to shift gears.

Step back for a beat. Push that big family reset button again, go back home to get the hugs we missed last time, get strong and healthy, and find our footing to start dreaming again.

If I don't sound sad about it, that's because if I know anything it's this:

When one big dream finds its sunset, another is just about to find its sunrise.

To be honest, I was really sad about this dream's sunset for a while. The truth is that we could have tried to push ourselves to make it work. We could have hidden our struggles and tried to turn our rain clouds into rainbows, but that just didn't feel right this time. We had to do what was right for our family. It's just part of being an adult, right?

And we chose to share this with you because, as a friend so wisely told me a few months ago, we all need to see the difficult side of living life on our own terms and going after our biggest dreams, too. We don't always need to see just the pie-in-the-sky moments; we need to see the pie that falls on the floor, too.

I've never been one to pack up and go home when things don't work out, but when I think about sharing our out-of-the-box life and talking with you about how to build big family togetherness, I have to tell you one thing:

Having people you can call your home is a big part of making big family dreams come true. They're the glue that holds our family together when things go sideways.

If you don't have a safety net of supportive family and friends rooting for you in your big family togetherness dreams, get one. If there's been hurt and abuse in your past, too much pain or brokenness, it doesn't have to be your biological family. Reach out and find family and friends wherever you are. That way, you always have people you can go home to when you need them the most.

With our home team cheering us on, sending us notes of encouragement and being there to love on us when we need to come back home for a bit, we can find the togetherness and adventure we're dreaming of. We'll get there!

Take a moment.

Think about what holds your family together when things go sideways on a big family dream. What stops you from reaching out for support? Who do you go to when you need a good talk and a hot cup of tea (and maybe even some banana pudding)?

Stop Making Excuses
(Step Up Again, Sister)

"I know it's hard, but you've got to step up again if you want the life you dream of."

It was a phrase that came to me from two wise women on opposite sides of the globe in the span of six months. Each time I heard it I knew I had to pay attention.

The first time it came from a big stage. I was living in Sydney, Australia, trying to make ends meet as a 26-year-old mom with two babies, nannying, cleaning houses, and trying to stretch every single dollar so that my hubby and I could soak up some learning at Hillsong College (him) and Hillsong Church (me). That Thursday morning was especially hard for me as both kids were cranky and I felt like the ugliest, frumpiest duckling on the planet, sitting in a giant auditorium listening to the speaker.

We were out of money and every opportunity was falling flat for us in Sydney. It was time to get out of school, go home to the States, and look for work, but the task seemed daunting and I didn't want to do any of it. I just wanted to take a nap and let someone else handle it for me. Bobbie Houston spoke that day about what it takes to step into the life we want and to be the woman, mom, sister, and daughter we were created to be.

I thought she would say God would take care of it if we just waited, but she didn't. Instead, she talked about how we all reach critical decision moments in our lives and we have to make the choice to step up again and again into something better, something greater, something we know we were created to do.

"I know it's hard," she said, "but you've got to step up again if you want the life you dream of."

The second time, just six months later, it came from my mom's dinner table back in the States. We had found a way to move home, and we were finding it difficult to get back on our feet. Mom had invited an old friend over for coffee, and since we were staying next door to her for a while, I wandered over to say hi. I was feeling torn and unsure that day, desperate for direction, and when I walked in the room and saw Rhonda Nobles, I could tell this was going to be more than coffee. Life, wisdom, and strength poured out of her like a fountain, so I couldn't help but seek her advice.

I told her about how I really wanted to stay home with my babies but I had been offered a great social justice job close by and we needed the money. I whined a little bit (okay, a lot) and said I didn't want my husband to get to stay home with the kids — I wanted to do that part myself. I didn't want to be a professional.

I just wanted to be a stay-at-home mom. I expected her to tell me that I needed to stick with my gut and stay home, that someone else would take care of all the rest, but she didn't. Instead, she talked about how, if we want to have the dreams in our hearts, we have to step up and make the hard choices sometimes.

"I know it's hard," she said, *"but you've got to step up again if you want the life you dream of."*

That same principle holds true for those of us looking for family togetherness and dreaming big dreams. It would be so much easier if we could just say a little prayer and magically have an instant, lasting connection with our spouse and kiddos, but it doesn't work that way. It would be so nice if we could just take a nap or dive into our work or get lost on Netflix and magically have the big family dreams we long for, but it doesn't work that way either.

If we want something more, we've got to step up again and again, no matter how many times we've stepped up before.

If we want our kids to be smart, strong, healthy, compassionate humans, we've got to step up, pay attention, make some sacrifices, and get them the tools they need to do that.

If we want to have a strong relationship with our spouses and kids, we've got to step up, pay attention, make some sacrifices, and work on building it.

If we want to travel more, work from home, work from the road, make a big life change, have a home our kids want to come back to when they're older, fight injustice, write a book, build a business, or accomplish any other big dream, we've got to step up, pay attention, make some sacrifices, and make it happen.

I know it's hard, but you've got to step up again if you want the life you dream of.

No excuses. You can do it.

Not because I've mastered this stepping up kind of life (I'm still working on it every single day) but because it's the only way forward.

Step up again, sister. You've got this.

And the next time you start thinking, "This is just too hard. I can't do it again" or "She's so lucky. I could never do that. My parents/husband/kids/personality is just too . . .," I hope you think about this togetherness tip and immediately know that you can do it. You can have the family togetherness and big dreams in your heart. You can step up again, no matter how many times you've stepped up before.

Take a moment.

Write your own stepping-up story. Have you ever had to do the hard work of stepping up to make things different for your family? What happened? Keep this around and read it the next time you need to step up again.

Get Outside

I've always loved getting outside with my family, and I'm always feeling like too many things keep me from doing it as often as I'd like. So when the coronavirus pandemic hit in the spring of 2020 and we were all required to stay home and change our way of life — I feel ridiculous for saying this — I started to feel trapped almost immediately. I knew I wasn't alone, so I wrote this tip in response.

We've been taking it easy this week in my family. At first, we tried to go on with homeschooling and working from home just like we always do, but it felt different — harder somehow. So we set about trying to turn *stuck at home* into *fun at home* by reading good books together, doing some out-of-the-box art projects, and watching a few educational videos about the pandemic and totally non-pandemic-related stuff too (like Jimmy Fallon's The Tonight Show At Home Edition — hilarious!).

We're not afraid, but we're taking this thing seriously and trying to do our best to help flatten the curve. It's crazy to think that the one simple act of staying home more can save thousands upon thousands of lives, but it can. I'm so encouraged to see so many people happy to do their part.

So why am I feeling trapped?

Probably because I'm so accustomed to going anywhere I want at the drop of a hat without even thinking about it, and because nearly a week into this thing, no one is saying how long we'll need to stay put.

The reality, though, is that we aren't trapped at all.

We can still do one thing that's huge for our health and a big boost for our family togetherness factor too — we can still get outside.

We can play in our backyards.

We can go hiking or biking.

We can toss a ball or chase a frisbee.

We can stargaze, people-watch, and build a campfire.

We can run, play, swing, play hopscotch, or just sit on our porches and sip tea.

I'll be honest with you — my family isn't there right now. We love the outdoors and have spent loads of time and money on quite a few epic outdoor adventures with our kiddos that have become such a big part of who we are as a family, but the rainy weather we've encountered lately has us waiting for bright sunny days that never seem to come. So, most days in March we've been getting out for just an hour or two and then going back to our to-do's. But being outside makes us come alive in ways that cuddling up on the couch by the TV just doesn't, and I've been wondering,

What kind of togetherness boost would happen if we got outside more regardless?

I know from experience it would be a big one, but in seasons of uncertainty, we have to be a little more intentional to make it happen.

If you follow me on Instagram, you already know that I've been completely swept away by a new book recently *The Call of the Wild + Free*, and just yesterday I dove into the chapter called "The School of Nature" where the author cites expert after expert to say in all sorts of ways, "Time in nature is not a luxury. It is a necessity." And I believe it.

Here are just a few:

"Compared to kids confined indoors, children who regularly play in nature show heightened motor control — including balance, coordination, and agility. They tend to engage more in imaginative and creative play, which in turn fosters language, abstract reasoning, and problem-solving skills, together with a sense of wonder." —*Scott Sampson (The Call of the Wild + Free)*

"The child should be taken daily, if possible, to scenes — moor or meadow, park, common, or shore — where he may find new things to examine, and so add to his store of real knowledge." — *Charlotte Mason*

"Everybody needs beauty as well as bread, places to play in and pray in, where nature may heal and give strength to body and soul." — *John Muir*

And if I know anything, it's that when we are at our best physically, mentally, spiritually, and emotionally, family togetherness naturally follows.

"Get outside. Get dirty. Start ooh-ing and aah-ing. Begin wondering and wandering again. Be afraid. Be adventurous. If you lead the way, I promise, before you know it, your children will be leading you". — *Ainsley Arment, The Call of the Wild + Free*

Take a moment.

What's your favorite thing to do outside with your crew? What stops you from doing it?

Conclusion

I Want More

"Restlessness is discontent, and discontent is the first necessity of progress. Show me a thoroughly satisfied man and I will show you a failure."

— *Thomas Edison*

The weird thing about family togetherness is that it's never accomplished. It's never done. We never graduate from it, and we'll never be thoroughly satisfied with it. We were made for connection, and we'll always long for it no matter what we do — big, small, or somewhere in between. The way I see it, we can either let that pile up on top of us and feel like a heavy weight of discontent, or we can let our hearts soar in knowing that every other human being on this planet is longing for belonging and connection just like we are — especially the humans who live in our houses and inhabit our family gatherings with us.

They want our attention, our hugs, our love. They want us just as much as we want them — no matter what kind of attitudes, words, or expressions might pop up from day to day.

And we've got some experience under our belts to help us connect with them — a few years of life lived, a few scraped knees, bee stings, and scruffed-up souls.

It all matters — every single thing we've been through, every single thing we've tried, and every job, every season, every conversation. Each one has taught us something and had a hand in bringing us to the very places where we stand today. Each decision, each step, each path we've taken in the past has led to this place — the place where we get to go after our big family dreams.

We may not know why everything happens in life or even why we make the life decisions we do, but they all make sense and add to our experience bank in the end. One example is how my family got into this whole homeschooling, full-time traveling, gypsy life and how those decisions led me to this place where I can share all of these stories with you now.

It started in 2009 when I felt something way down deep in my soul telling me that homeschooling preschool was important for my family. It made no sense, but I tried it anyway. Four years later, homeschooling made it possible for my family to travel full-time with just a few weeks' preparation, and now seven more years down the track, I can see how critical and therapeutic learning at home has been for the unique adventures and struggles we've faced as a family. From helping our kids manage anxiety and explore a passion for art, history, science, and literature to giving us parents a second childhood where we get to experience wonder and awe in seeing parts of the world we've only dreamt of before, traveling and homeschooling is our jam.

What's yours?

I bet you either have a good story about how you found it or some big dreams in your heart about a few ways you're looking.

As this book comes to a close, I want you to know beyond a shadow of a doubt that just by reading these words, you're already ahead of the game when it comes to family togetherness, even if it doesn't feel like it — especially if it doesn't feel like it. You have everything you need to build strong, deep, lasting connection into the very fabric of your family's lifestyle and DNA just because you're you and you have this desire within you.

You can do this, and if you want more than you've got right now, that's actually a good thing.

You can brainstorm your own togetherness tips, make a list of what works for your family and keep it where everyone can see it. Write down your biggest family dreams and start thinking about what it would take to make them happen. You can hop into our email group at togethernessredefined.com/subscribe and get a new togetherness tip every Friday morning to spark your creativity, too.

You can make friends who are on this same path so that you don't it alone; stay connected with other families who are doing this thing right along with you.

As I said at the beginning of this book, I believe that parents are the leaders of family togetherness and the best possible outcomes for our children. We are the answer. You, my friend, are the answer.

Keep reading, researching, finding ideas, and giving them a go. There are more ideas, tools, and resources where these togetherness tips came from, and the internet is filled with families who are building a foundation of togetherness and going after their dreams. Find your tribe of encouragers and stick with them.

If you're still looking for your tribe, we'd love to have you try out our Togetherness Redefined community. It's fun, free, and filled with a boost for your family-loving soul every single week. You can hop in today at togethernessredefined.com. I'll see you there!

And no matter who you choose to walk this path alongside, my biggest hope for you is that you keep going. Keep trying. Keep showing up for your family. In a few years when we're all older, grayer, and wiser, we'll be thanking our former selves for putting in the work. I know we will.

Afterword

One More Thing

"Do what you feel in your heart to be right, for you'll be criticized anyway."
— *Eleanor Roosevelt*

"Stay away from negative people; they have a problem for every solution."
— *Albert Einstein*

I'm the kind of mama who always puts a P.S. and sometimes a P.P.S. at the end of a letter, so I couldn't end this book without sending you one more note.

Don't be mistaken; this way of life that you've now chosen will not be without opposition. On the path to redefining togetherness for your family, you will encounter criticism. You will experience heartache. You will even lose touch with some people and may even have to walk away from some relationships to make it happen. And when that happens, I want you to remember the two quotes at the top of this page. They've taught me that we can't sacrifice what's right for us because we're afraid of being criticized — we're going to be criticized either way — and that we can't waste our lives hanging out with negative people or sharing our good ideas with them — they'll never see the possibilities we do.

It seems odd that anyone would criticize us for prioritizing family togetherness, doesn't it? It seems counterintuitive that we would have to walk away from some relationships to make other relationships stronger. It seems just plain weird that anyone would be negative about a family making time to be together and doing life in a way that makes being together easier for us.

It seems strange to me, too, but it happens to me all the time, and I know it will happen to you too.

Here's why — It's actually easier to talk about something than it is to do it. It's easier to call a friend on the phone and complain that you can't get it all together than it is to take a deep breath and get it all together. It's somehow more soothing to pray and pray and pray for something to happen than it is to move forward and make it happen with shaky knees and a prayer on every breath.

So, when you start making changes in your family and prioritizing family time, family travel, or big family dreams over gossipy phone calls, nights out with the girls, and the busyness and expectation of traditional life, criticism will come.

Rejection will come, too.

But you can handle it, especially now that you know it's coming. You can find new friends, ones who are also all about redefining togetherness. (I find these on social media, chat with them weekly, and meet up with them all over the country!) These are the kind of friends that make our souls sing. They help us be the mamas we've always wanted to be. They help us make our families stronger. And they help us find the words to say to old friends that might even help them build a friendship with the new us. Some of them will, but not all of them.

At the end of the day, no matter who criticizes us or who tries to solve all of our solutions with their problems, we can redefine togetherness for our families. We can have the big family dreams that have been in our hearts for years.

You can totally do this, and I'll be right here cheering you along, answering your questions, and shouting it from the rooftops when you have wins — the big ones and the small ones, too.

If you're looking for a few new family-loving friends, grab a coffee and a computer and join our community of mamas today at togethernessredefined.com/subscribe. We'd love to have you.

I'll see you there!

Acknowledgments

The fact that you're holding this book in your hands still astounds me. I can't believe it's made its way out of my notebook, off of my computer screen, and into your home. Without the people listed below, it would still be only a dream.

Matthew, who makes my life an adventure, deserves more credit than he ever receives, and loves me for my many quirks, you've put up with way too many hours of my distraction and prattling on about book writing, gone on way too many solo grocery runs, and listened to way too many of my ramblings to help me see this dream come true. You are my favorite.

Elijah and Malachi, who inspire every single word, who make me happy just by being in this world, and who go along with their parents' crazy ideas with big smiles, you continually inspire and challenge me with your intelligence, creativity, and spark. I love you more than I can say, and I'll always be your biggest fan.

Mom and Dad, who saw this day coming 38 years ago and never let me forget how much they believed in me and how proud they were, even on my lowest days. Mom, I know you're reading this in heaven; and Dad, let me get you a discount on those 200 copies you're buying for your friends.

Dee and Azia, Harmony, Easton, and Cohen, who put up

with so much from me and love me regardless.

Matthew's family, who saw me as their own a long time ago and cheer me on in so many ways.

Kristen, who asked that fateful question in 2015, "Do you write?" and has been feeding the dream ever since.

Camille, who encouraged me, cheered me on, and edited her heart out for this book.

Melissa, who asked about this book every chance she got and never failed to read drafts, encourage me, and inspire so many good ideas.

Jacki, who reminded me why I write.

Liz and the artists at Unsplash, for sharing their photography talents for the cover.

Every mama who responded to a togetherness tip email, commented on a post, asked a question, or sent an encouraging word my way: Priska, Jenn, April, Jessica, Karlee, Laura, Mindy, Sherry, Maggie, Lisa, Ashley, Susan, Toni, Sunny, Jane, Windy, Dianne, Tish, Joy, Paige, Jess, Alyssa, Donna, ReKasa, Hannah, Shelley, Jamie, Lesley, and so many more. I see you. I appreciate every single encouraging word. They matter more than you know.

The mamas on the internet who taught me that big things are possible with small chunks of time and just how much we all need each other on this great big adventure called motherhood: Kara, Cait, Sarah, Jamie, and so many more. Without you making the way, there wouldn't have been a way for this book. Thank you for what you do for mamas every single day.

The ladies in my life who don't have children of their own but who never let that stop them from encouraging, inspiring, and loving like a mother does: Susan, Sam, Sue, Ruthie, and others – you are so important to me. Don't ever let anyone tell you you're not a mama.

The teachers and authors who poured life into me with their words, stories, lessons, and classes: Marie, Sandra, Gail, Julie, Anne, Elise, Madeline, Ainsley, Shauna, Sarah, and so many others who have impacted my life as mentors, writers, guides, and way-makers, I hope you recognize your wisdom in these pages. With every word I wrote, I was reminded that what people say about writers is true – every writer is a lover of good books and good teaching, determined to let the ripples of influence received from another good writer and teacher flow out from herself. That's me, and those good writers and teachers are you.

You, sweet reader, who are investing in yourself and your family's big dreams and who saw the potential for all of those things in these pages. Thank you.

Others, so many others, who have crossed my path, impacted my life, and influenced stories that found their way into this book. I'm certain that after I've hit publish, I will inevitably remember someone whose name should be printed here. If that's you, please forgive me. I'm making a list for my next book, and I'm convinced that by the time I write enough books to fill a few shelves I will have been able to thank all of the people who have made them all possible. Thank you for believing in me in a way that makes that dream a very real possibility.

And God, Who holds it all, gives it all, and has so much more for us than we could ever imagine.

Come say hi!

If you found your way to this first book of mine, I would love to hear your family's story and what led you to pick up a copy for yourself. Use the tag #togethernessredefinedbook on social media or tag @celeste__orr on Instagram to get in touch.

And if you loved the book, leave a review on Amazon to help other mamas find their way to these pages too.

Are you a writer, too?

Some people were born into families of writers and readers and seem to be destined to publish books and beautiful blogs from a young age. I was not. My dad was a talented mechanic, my mom an accountant and secretary, my sister was into music, and the only one going to the library looking for a fun book on a Saturday in my house was me. But they believed in me and told me I could do anything I set my mind to — even write books. And that changed everything.

If you need someone to believe in you and equip you with courage, inspiration, and step-by-step guidance for making your writing dreams come true, you might just love our *Mamas Who Write* group. Grab the details at celesteorr.com.

Made in the USA
Columbia, SC
30 July 2020